THE EXCEPTIONAL
LEADER

THE EXCEPTIONAL LEADER

How Smart Leaders Produce SMART RESULTS

Bob Shirley

Published by
Rupa Publications India Pvt. Ltd 2022
7/16, Ansari Road, Daryaganj
New Delhi 110002

Sales centres:
Bengaluru Chennai
Hyderabad Jaipur Kathmandu
Kolkata Mumbai Prayagraj

Copyright © Bob Shirley 2022

The views and opinions expressed in this book are the author's own and the facts are as reported by him which have been verified to the extent possible, and the publishers are not in any way liable for the same.

All rights reserved.
No part of this publication may be reproduced, transmitted, or stored in a retrieval system, in any form or by any means, electronic, mechanical, photocopying, recording or otherwise, without the prior permission of the publisher.

ISBN: 978-81-291-4006-7

Seventh impression 2025

10 9 8 7

The moral right of the author has been asserted.

Printed in India

This book is sold subject to the condition that it shall not, by way of trade or otherwise, be lent, resold, hired out, or otherwise circulated, without the publisher's prior consent, in any form of binding or cover other than that in which it is published.

CONTENTS

Introduction   *vii*

1. Leadership Today   1
2. The Remarkable Leader   14
3. Style Your Own Leadership   26
4. Adapt to (Survive) Thrive   39
5. Two Sides of the Same Coin: Management and Leadership   52
6. Manage Your Management Better   64
7. Speak Up (Like a Boss)   78
8. You Are Your Own Statement   98
9. Authority vs *True* Leadership   111
10. Have a Say, Sway Them Away   127
11. Leading Future Leaders   138
12. Create a Culture They Fall in Love With   151
13. The Post-Pandemic Leader: Your Brand-New Leadership Style   169

INTRODUCTION

*As we look ahead to the next century,
leaders will be those who empower others.*

—Bill Gates

Leaders have been our superheroes since day-one. We all have leaders we have been crazy about. We try to mimic their way of talking, their way of walking, their way of dressing, their way of thinking, but mostly, we want to be loved and admired like them; we want to achieve the unachievable, we want to work well with others, we want to be *accepted* by others and we want to leave our marks. Am I right? Thought so!

Knowingly or unknowingly, our world has been under the influence of some great business giants. Be it Elon Musk, Mark Zuckerberg, Bill Gates, Jeff Bezos or Steve Jobs, these genius minds have achieved some unimaginable things, and it wasn't just their genius but also their *brilliant* leadership skills. After all, a lone genius can only do so much; the real genius knows very well how he's going to create his loyal team—his corporate empire.

Every human has an urge to lead, inspire and gain success in tasks. It could be in your day-to-day function as a homemaker, a student, or a manager distributing and directing numerous responsibilities in an organization. Within each of us is a leader who strives to push limits and set examples. But leadership isn't easy—leaders must possess the traits that will help them achieve in their respective fields. To fulfil your desire to lead and bring a change, you need to know how to lead—and how to lead well at that. And that's *exactly* what this book will teach you! Let's begin by getting a deeper understanding of leadership, shall we?

Everyone knows what leadership is, but few people can tell what it *truly* means. We talk about leaders and leadership nearly every day (even in the business world), but have you ever tried to actually define leadership? It can be much harder than you may think, but taking the time to define leadership becomes important for you to seek the leader within you. Everyone's view of leadership is different, and that's what makes the role of a leader so interesting and unique. The way you lead is so different from that of your father's or your friend Paul's, yet all of you can be successful in your own ways.

Also, know that you don't have to be a political giant or Tim Cooks to be a leader. There will be times in your life when you must stand up as a leader, whether you are in college or entering the workforce. Even if you're not in a leadership position, there will be times in your life when you'll need to use your leadership skills to help those around you—whether it's dealing with a crisis among your friends if you all miss a flight or working out new dinner plans with your siblings when your kitchen is a disaster and your mother isn't available. Yes, that is a form of leadership as well!

A true leader does way more than just giving orders and managing those under him. He pushes the people in his team to reach their highest potentials. He creates a loyal army through his charm, intelligence and genuine care for his people—as well as his company.

By being a true leader, you show others that you can inspire and motivate your team for the betterment of the company. Setting yourself apart as this type of leader will require having certain qualities that establish trust and respect within your team. True leadership, then, becomes a representation of the way you work with your team to achieve goals and work efficiently. A true leader leads by example and establishes strong bonds with all his teammates to ensure success for all—without leaving anyone out.

Leadership is a behaviour that can be learnt, and this learnt skill becomes natural and automatic over time. Most of us wonder *how on earth* leaders know how to make the best decisions—often under immense pressure. In moments of sheer crisis, how do they not crumple? How do they remain so calm? How are they not murdered by their workers for making such difficult decisions?

The confidence of these leaders to make these decisions comes from thousands of experiences and encounters teamed up with *hundreds* of situations, personality types and unforeseen failures.

That is exactly why the most successful leaders we know are instinctual decision makers. Having done it so many times throughout their careers, they become immune to the pressures and stress that comes with taking massive decisions and extremely intuitive about what lies ahead of these decisions. This is why most senior executives will tell you they depend strongly upon their 'gut-feeling' when making difficult decisions at a moment's notice. Isn't that crazy? Well, you can possess this gut-feeling too. Read on to find out how.

Just like the big empires in our history, businesses rise and fall as the times change. Similarly, some stay at the top for a long time, while others fade away after a few years. Great leadership is the key to long-term, sustainable success. A strong business leader can inspire people, have a clear vision that others can believe in and lead the organization's innovation. Investors, consumers and employees will all want to buy in when outstanding leaders are in charge.

There's no greater, more fascinating story out there than

the history of business itself. If you find yourself wanting to model your business style off of the successful business leaders from decades gone by, consider these business giants I've listed below; they've all changed the world, in one way or another, building unshakable profit-making empires.

Henry Ford	The inventor of the Model T not only introduced engines but also a more efficient way of working through his Model T assembly line. This method of production reduced the cost of materials and the final product, changing the accessibility of American vehicles and the world around him. Changing the course of history truly pays.
Madam C.J. Walker	The most brilliant business leaders identify an underserved market segment and fill it; no one exhibits this better than Madam C.J. Walker. Walker created hair care products in the late nineteenth and early twentieth centuries that specifically addressed the requirements of a demographic typically disregarded by conventional American beauty companies: African-American women. Her company grew rapidly, and she swiftly established herself as one of the most successful American businesswomen in history.
Steve Jobs	He didn't invent the wheel, but he certainly reinvented it—the computer—to make it more accessible and intriguing to the rest of the world. Steve Jobs, Apple Inc.'s distinctive face, is a name familiar to millions, and his technology has an impact on millions more.
Bill Gates	As you most probably already know, Gates founded Microsoft, the world's largest PC software company; and each year, he is consistently near the top of the list of the world's wealthiest people. Over the years, Gates has slowly transitioned away from Microsoft and into philanthropic ventures. His foundation, Bill & Melinda Gates Foundation, is working to provide clean water and sanitation (among other things) to third-world countries. Like Warren Buffett, Gates has also promised to leave the vast majority of his wealth to charity.

Jeff Bezos	(Does he even need an introduction at this point?) Jeff Bezos is most known for being the creator of the international mega-corporation Amazon. He was formally the person to take Bill Gates' place as the world's richest man. Despite the fact that Amazon is now the world's largest corporation, the company had relatively humble origins. Jeff Bezos established Amazon in his garage in 1994. What began as a small online bookstore quickly grew into a major e-commerce force. Amazon now ships to more than 50 countries and daily distributes millions of unique products. Despite the fact that Amazon started small, Jeff Bezos had the vision and drive to revolutionize the e-commerce industry and expand his company into the world's largest enterprise.
Elon Musk	You'll find his name *everywhere*—from social media, to television and magazines! Musk is most widely known for his founding of PayPal, SpaceX and his heavy involvement in Tesla Motors. His vision and passion for pushing the boundaries of technology and consumer integration have led to increased exposure to solar power, high-speed transportation and artificial intelligence.
Larry Page and Sergey Brin	Page and Brin were both PhD students at Stanford University when they worked on something that has possibly had a greater impact on society than anyone else on our list. They started Google in 1998, a fairly basic search engine that would soon transform the internet landscape. The search engine became more powerful and accurate as it expanded in popularity. 'Just Google it,' became a widespread slogan soon after, as people realized they could discover almost anything using the search engine. Every day, Google receives about 3.5 billion searches. To put that figure into context, Google is responsible for over 92 per cent of all internet searches. Brin and Page both had exceptional intuition when it came to seeing the true potential of what they were developing and how it would completely research the internet and society.

Warren Buffett	Buffett is one of the world's most successful investors. He has been dubbed the 'Wizard of Omaha' (his hometown is Omaha, Nebraska), and he is consistently listed as one of the world's wealthiest individuals. He has also promised to donate nearly all of his wealth to humanitarian organizations after he dies.
Tim Cook	Steve Jobs is a hard act to follow, but Tim Cook is doing a fantastic job so far! Cook is shaping the future with his own creative innovations, rather than seeking to match consumer-facing developments. 'You kind of want to handle a technological company like you're in the dairy business. You've got a problem if it's past its freshness date,' he once said. He has undoubtedly contributed to Apple's consumer products remaining dynamic and relevant.
Mark Zuckerberg	(Another iconic figure who doesn't need much of an introduction.) Zuckerberg launched Facebook from his Harvard University dormitory room on February 4, 2004. College roommates and fellow Harvard students Eduardo Saverin, Andrew McCollum, Dustin Moskovitz and Chris Hughes assisted Zuckerberg in creating Facebook. The group then introduced Facebook to other college campuses—and the rest is history! Facebook expanded rapidly, reaching one billion users by 2012. Since 2010, *Time* magazine has named Zuckerberg among the 100 wealthiest and most influential people in the world. In December 2016, *Forbes* ranked Zuckerberg 10th on *Forbes*' list of 'The World's Most Powerful People'.

However, don't get intimidated by the names above; they all had humble beginnings—yes, I know it's hard to imagine—but these corporate demi-gods were ordinary chaps, *just like us.* Leadership isn't limited to billionaires or the politically powerful, and that's something you must always remember. Leadership is an attitude and a quality—rather than a fixed, static position. That's what makes it so unique and powerful. With effort and tactics, anyone can be an exceptional leader!

A business leader is anyone who is able to motivate a group of people in order to achieve a common goal in a company. This can be someone in a position of power, like a vice president, chief executive officer of a major company or the editor-in-chief of a newspaper. It can also be someone lower on the ladder, like a team leader or a sales associate. In other words, you don't have to be a billionaire or a CEO to be a leader. Anyone, with the right skills, regardless of their position in a company or organization, can be a business leader. Exciting, isn't it?

Now, let me make it clear, there is a difference between leadership and management (more on which I'll elaborate in Chapter 2). Similarly, there is a difference between leadership and *outstanding* leadership. The point to note here is that leaders and managers differ in a number of crucial ways. For instance, leadership is all about having a vision and then actualizing it through a sense of mission, whereas management is all about day-to-day execution of plans. Of course, leaders need to be excellent managers as well, since leadership is as much about 20,000-foot view of the organization as it is about on the ground execution.

Having said that, there are again differences between leaders, and outstanding and transformational leaders. Whereas all organizations and nations, as well as societies, have an abundance of leaders, there are only a *few* instances in time when truly outstanding and transformational leaders arrive on the world stage (as I've listed for you above).

In addition, while all organizations do boast of a stable set of leaders, there are only some organizations that have the chance to witness transformational leadership. For instance, why did Microsoft and Apple become such profit monsters while other technology firms continue to show record profits but aren't even mentioned in discussions or books?

The difference here is that both Microsoft and Apple were

founded by truly extraordinary people, who not only had a vision but were also willing to stake their personalities on turning that vision into a reality. Also, both Microsoft and Apple were firms that were highly innovative and inventive thanks to the calibre and potential of Gates and Jobs. Thus, it is indeed the case that leadership and transformational leadership are two different aspects that must be noted if one were to make sense of why not all organizations achieve greatness.

Production in any organization or business is concerned with land, labour, capital and entrepreneurship—as we all are generally aware of. But who brings these forces together? It is *the exceptional leader.*

Leadership is the major factor that makes everything work together seamlessly. Without leadership, all other business resources are ineffective. New-age business leaders are aware of the concerns of their employees and are on top of new developments—in the market and in the desires of their beloved consumers. There are several styles of leaders; some prefer to delegate to their personnel while others want to work together. It's always a good idea to tap into your employees' creativity: if they have a wonderful idea that could boost the company's earnings, why not use it? Facilitative leaders, on the other hand, outsource the majority of responsibilities to their subordinates and spend time equipping their staff with the tools they need to succeed in their jobs. The distinctive leadership style of the CEO-in-charge determines the organization's culture, i.e., leaders define the company and its culture by their practises, visions and tactics.

In business, the leader is self-assured, relentless and creative. He or she has the ability to start a new firm and will devote all of their energy to its success. Furthermore, one of their distinguishing characteristics is their ability to inspire others. The leader is an excellent communicator. They know exactly how to put company policies into action, and they work hard to achieve success. They know how to create objectives and work to achieve them as rapidly as possible. This flexible approach to achieving their objectives enables them to grow and promote their company quickly. But most importantly, they know how to get people on their bandwagon through their charm, communication and humility. The exceptional leaders are always exceptional persons—first and foremost.

Think you have the appropriate leadership skills? Fill this table and find out for yourself:

	Questions	Always (1)	Often (2)	Sometimes (3)	Rarely (4)	Never (5)
1.	If I am in a leadership position, I state clearly the goals that others should be working towards.					
2.	People tell me that I am easy to talk to.					
3.	Before giving feedback to someone else, I would try to see things from his or her point of view.					
4.	When employees have worked extra hard, I believe they should be encouraged and rewarded.					
5.	I maintain a positive attitude even when things look bad in the workplace.					
6.	I manage to persuade someone to see my point of view instead of forcing it on them.					
7.	People look to me to help maintain hope when things go wrong in the organization. I don't crumple under pressure and am able to make sound decisions.					
8.	I've been told I'm very organized and efficient with my tasks.					

9.	Once we have reached one goal, I set my sights on the next one for my organization.					
10.	Working in teams excites me. The synergy always leads to innovation and success.					

- If you've scored a 10 (without any delusion or cheating), you're a good leader! Read more to find out how to be an *exceptional* leader, who births other leaders and changes the game.
- If you've scored a 50, well, you've obviously opened a book that you desperately need.
- If you're somewhere in between (and I am guessing you must be), continue reading to master the art of leadership—irrespective of who you are in your company.

Takeaways

- Nobody's born an exceptional leader; you train yourself to be one.
- Great leaders not only transform themselves but transform whole societies, nations and obviously, organizations.
- Being a good leader might make you successful, but being a great leader is what really makes you transformational.
- Your business is reduced to nothing without interactive, efficient and collaborative leadership.
- Leadership is a learnt strategy that becomes a part of how you function at the workplace over time.

I

LEADERSHIP TODAY

The true mark of a leader is the willingness to stick with a bold course of action—an unconventional business strategy, a unique product-development roadmap, a controversial marketing campaign—even as the rest of the world wonders why you're not marching in step with the status quo. In other words, real leaders are happy to zig while others zag. They understand that in an era of hyper-competition and non-stop disruption, the only way to stand out from the crowd is to stand for something special.[1]

—Bill Taylor, writer, entrepreneur and thinker

I ask you again: what is leadership to you? Think hard, this is going to be the main basis of this chapter. While you think, let me tell you a little about what a modern, exceptional leader is.

Jacob Morgan discloses that as part of his research for his new book *The Future Leader*, he spoke with over 140 CEOs

---

[1] Bill Taylor, 'Do You Pass the Leadership Test?', *Harvard Business Review*, 3 August 2010, https://hbr.org/2010/08/pass-leadership-test, Accessed on 16 March 2022.

from around the world and asked them to define leadership.[2] Because it's a word we use so often without fully articulating it, many individuals struggled or had to pause to ponder. We take leadership for granted, assuming that we all understand what it is and what makes a great leader, but there is no clear, straightforward answer! The CEOs' answers presented an important story once they identified their definitions. Morgan didn't get a single duplicate response out of over 140 people. Why? Because there are no hard-and-fast rules to being the exceptional leader.

Some CEOs defined leadership as having business skills—like setting a vision or achieving goals for a company. Other people focused on human qualities like empathy, humility or diversity. Every answer was different, but they were *all* correct. Every leader has their own personal definition of leadership, which influences how they lead, the culture and direction of their company. The definition of leadership can also change as the leaders themselves change. With new leaders come new approaches to leadership which impacts overall cultures, employees and organizations.

Summing up the main points from all of their definitions, Morgan states, 'A leader is someone who can see how things can be improved and who rallies people to move toward that better vision. Leaders can work toward making their vision a reality while putting people first. Just being able to motivate people isn't enough—leaders need to be empathetic and connect with people to be successful. Leaders don't have to come from the same background or follow the same path. Future leaders will actually be more diverse, which brings a variety of perspectives. Of course, other people could disagree with my definition. The

---

[2]Jacob Morgan, *The Future Leader,* Wiley, 2020.

most important thing is that organizations are united internally with their definition of leadership.'[3]

Leadership in a Rapidly Transforming World

Your standard mobile phone nowadays contains a thousand times more computing power than all of NASA's computers in 1969—which helped send people to the moon. And it's more than a million times cheaper. That's weird to imagine, isn't it? It is just one of many examples illustrating how the fourth industrial (or first digital) revolution has radically changed the world we live in.

In a world of constant changes where technology dictates how we live every single day and social issues are being prioritized, leaders need to step up and show the way forward. CEOs are being pressured to take a position on social issues; C-suite executives are being asked to work more collaboratively. The new leader cannot walk alone; he must always walk with a pack—with *his* pack.

Our world is undergoing massive, disruptive changes at a topsy-turvy speed. Innovation, digitalization and technological progress are transforming whole industries, reshaping the minds of consumers and challenging traditional leadership styles. This demands a new approach to leadership and business strategy—one where inspiring leaders replace strict business plans with an ambitious dream, where the focus shifts from results towards performance and employees' well-being, and where *reinvention is embraced.*

The world in which we live in is also increasingly becoming more interconnected. Whole societies, economies and political systems are becoming more intertwined as millions of products

---

[3]Ibid.

and services are exchanged in mere seconds. Companies are continuously having to adapt to these changes, else they are out of the business game pretty quick. In fact, what worked yesterday may not even work today—thanks to globalization.

There is no doubt that this very globalization has impacted how leadership is practised by all. For example, leadership skills and practises which are effective in one country may be useless in another due to differences in cultural believes and values. Therefore, it is important to understand how leadership can be used to effectively lead in a globalized environment.

Leadership, in today's world, requires new values altogether. No longer is a leader simply a person who can make a good and inspiring speech. Today, a leader faces challenges of huge political, economic and environmental proportions. A leader should have the ability to convince followers (and others) to change destructive habits, to be good communicators, to focus more on the participation of women in leadership roles and to encourage the use of cutting-edge technology in the office. To thrive in these times of great uncertainty, the best leaders lead through influence, not the power of their position. The 'command-and-control' ways of the past are gone. The days of simply telling someone to do something are gone too. Basically, the exceptional leader's job is one of never-ending negotiation and persuasion (as tiring as that sounds)—based on mutual trust and respect. That is not easy nor is it simple, but with a little bit of practise and determination, you can be the future exceptional leader your office is so hungry for.

Some points to keep in mind to become an exceptional leader:

- **A leader today must listen to and hear everyone's ideas and suggestions (including the youths).** Michael McKinney, in an article called 'Questions Are the Answers' stated, 'Great leaders are great at asking better questions. In the rapidly changing environment we are in today, it is imperative. Our future depends on it. Until you ask different questions, you can't innovate. Breakthroughs require different questions from the ones we've been asking.'[4]

- It is becoming clear that **traditional performance management isn't sufficient anymore.** In times of unpredictability and constant change, trying to precisely plan, measure and control results is inadequate. The focus must shift from planning to innovation, experimentation and development. The most effective leaders are able to perceive and appreciate the big picture. Some could argue that good leaders have always been able to do so. But keep in mind that the image itself has changed. The canvas is significantly bigger, more complicated and more flexible.
- As speed becomes our main driver, **companies need to become increasingly agile, dynamic and adaptable.** To enable that, **leaders need to empower their most valuable resource: their employees.** External rewards (such as bonuses) are, at best, a temporary motivation now. True motivation and engagement arise from finding the work you do meaningful.
- To empower their gems, **leaders need to coach.** Lou Holtz was a famous coach. He once said that coaching is like driving a bus; you can have only one driver at a time. If you don't like the driver, you get off the bus. If you want to be the driver, I will throw you off the bus.

---

[4]Michael McKinney, 'Questions Are the Answers', Leadership Now, 19 December 2018, https://www.leadershipnow.com/leadingblog/2018/12/questions_are_the_answer.html, Accessed on 16 March 2022.

Leaders are like bus drivers, but they're not the sole drivers; followers are the equal go-getters of success. Followers get on the bus, and they go where the bus driver takes them. But they (the followers) *make the decision* to get on the bus. The leader projects whatever the followers are looking to follow, but it is the followers who create the potential for the leader to make the best out of his leadership by coaching. Basically, there is no sole leader in a business—a good leader coaches and creates other drivers. This works well, especially in times of crisis. Imagine how good you'd feel if your kids could also drive when you were half-asleep, trying to drop them to school. You'd know there wouldn't be an accident even if you fell asleep, because you'd taught your kids to handle the situation and drive the car instead.

- Leaders must now possess **the ability to make decisions quickly**, despite utter chaos and uncertainty. In this era of globalization and technological innovation, the boundaries that used to distinguish industries and companies are blurring. Real-time competition is a reality, and honestly, it's *the only reality*. The new leaders no longer have the luxury of long planning, and he is more than okay with that.
- Moreover, **leaders should ensure that everyone is put in a role to succeed and create team spirit** between individuals, teams and departments for more far-reaching better solutions. Also, a leader needs to well-versed with all the departments of his team. My dad tells me he remembers the days when, if you excelled at finance, your chances of making it to the top were better than those of your colleagues in other departments. You did not have to understand marketing—an agency handled that. You didn't really have to talk to customers—the sales representatives handled that. And you did not have to worry about what was happening in another

industry. Chances are, those events would have absolutely no impact on your company.

That is not the case today. The new-age exceptional leader cannot afford to stay safely tucked away in his cosy, air-conditioned cabin. He must understand how the different parts of his business work. He must know how to beat his competition. And for that, he needs to get outside his office and talk and listen to employees, customers, stakeholders, investors—basically, everyone becomes an important asset.

- **New leaders lead, follow and get out of the way.** I remember seeing a poster with that headline on it once. I believe there were cowboys in it, charging towards the camera. As you observed the bunch (perhaps a posse) riding, arms waving, horses panting, and very dusty, dust was all around them. But the headline sums up leadership perfectly: you either lead, follow, or get out of the way.

  Leadership is one of those words that has no meaning by itself. It's impenetrable. You can't really touch, feel or hear it, much less define it, like you can't truly touch, feel, or hear 'trust' or 'love'. You have the potential to be a leader. Is this, however, a sign that you are no longer a follower? Respectfully, a leader has amassed a following of people who, for whatever reason, believes in the same things as the leader. Leaders issue orders, and followers carry them out. As a result, in order to have a leader, followers must possess the trait of obedience. It is also a quality that a leader expects and requires in order to be a leader. There are no followers if they do not obey. There is no leader without supporters. See the connection?

- To understand what is really going on, both inside and outside their companies, **the best leaders accept new ideas, criticisms and different perspectives.** They ensure they get the right information, not a sugar-coated, pretty version of events. No-one, including your employees or partners, likes to admit that they made a mistake. It is natural to sugar-coat the bad news. But if you do not have all the facts and the truth, how can you solve the problem?

- Twenty-first century leadership is viewed as a property of any social network. Not solely the domain of those 'in charge', **leadership is something in which *everyone* participates.** This new definition of leadership incorporates a full spectrum of values and fosters a wide range of capacities, competencies and skills. These include, but are not limited to: critical, creative and systems like thinking, self-awareness, communication and dialogue, social and cultural intelligence, and facilitation of team and collaborative processes.

What Are Some Ways You Move Towards Being a Magnetic Twenty-First Century Leader?

1) **Embrace and Encourage Diversity:** Different perspectives are preferable to more of the same. Better agility necessitates organizations finding the greatest individuals, regardless of location, for various perspectives. This includes not just differences in genders and nations, but also differences in experiences, generations and viewpoints. Remember that a salad is finest when it's loaded with a variety of vegetables, cheeses and sauces?

2) **Serve and Serve More:** In the Information Age, everyone, everywhere is potentially in a relationship with you (whether you choose it or not). A service mentality is not just an ethical plus—it's *required*. Your workers serve you, but you also serve them, irrespective of organizational hierarchies. In Myles Munroe's words, 'Great leaders do not desire to

lead but to serve.'
3) **Don't Fear Change, Be the Change:** The nature of leadership itself is evolving. We are moving from authority to trust; from hierarchy to networking; from decision-making to inspiration; and from power to self-awareness. Learning how to manage your behaviour is central to developing leadership fit for a dynamic, unpredictable future. Just know you can ride through the wave when it booms at you instead of running away from it. All exceptional leaders do that.
4) **Envision:** As visionaries, leaders shape the emergence of a clear goal and vision—a North Star—that resonates throughout their business and beyond it. See it as a silent war-cry!

    They don't arrive at this in the boardroom. Rather, they emerge from the organization by observing and listening to people *throughout* the system, offering ideas for consideration and integrating others' perspectives with their own original thinking.
5) **Achieve Through Teams and Technology:** As visionaries, leaders also work with teams and gadgets to translate the vision into actual success.

    It's only a matter of time before humans and technology merge and work together to get the job done. Being adaptable and staying up-to-date on the latest technology is key when it comes to leading a business into a time of continuous innovation and uncertainty.
6) **Be the Architect of Your Organization:** Along with making plans, leaders must also build the organization as an open and empowered system capable of continuously planning, executing, and adjusting resource flow across shorter working cycles in order to achieve its goals. They prefer a more in-depth investigation of the organization's system designs,

which allows them to re-imagine how things are produced or sales are created. To allow new kinds of business and organizational models to emerge, it is necessary to let go of limiting assumptions and beliefs.

7) **Prioritize Communication:** As a leader, communication is an integral element of your job. Communication skills are not something that can be delegated or outsourced. Your message is you. Effective twenty-first century leaders must grasp an ever-evolving variety of communication demands, from new media to traditional gatherings.

8) **Gather Knowledge From *Wherever* You Find It:** What are you learning from various generations? Every generation now has a voice. Will you listen and learn? Similarly, a world of customers, competitors, prospects and resources is just a mouse click away. Communicate and collaborate where they are—not where *you* are. This truly helps you achieve a globalized perspective.

9) **Lead Equally Well Remotely:** With the advent of the pandemic and all of the updates to technology, many jobs are no longer full-time salaried positions, and they can be done remotely, anywhere in the world. Contractors seem to be the way of the future, and as long as they have a laptop and Wi-Fi, they can likely get the job done for you. However, you must figure out a way to manage all of these people on their schedules and in their respective time zones. Organizing all of these people can be daunting, but it can be a huge asset in the future.

10) **Set an Example:** It is important to lead by example. Be open and honest with your clients and staff, and collaborate with your co-workers to achieve success. This will earn the organization's respect for your leadership style, as well as a high level of trust in you and your team.

11) **Aim To Be the Best in a Competitive World:** That's right, *in the whole world!* With today's globalized competition, mediocrity is lethal. 'Best in the world' is the only sustainable business model. In our digital age, people can seek out the best value from anywhere in the world. Resting on laurels or settling for second-best is only for mediocre leaders.

12) **Adapt To Survive:** The value of your service is determined by your capacity to evolve in the rapidly unfolding circumstances of the early twenty-first century. Nonetheless, don't kid yourself into thinking that your transformation issues are unprecedented. They haven't yet reached the level of those born around the turn of the twentieth century, for example. In Leon Megginson words, 'It's not the strongest or the most intelligent who survive but those most adaptive to change. Over the past 10 years, the need for, and focus on, adaptability has accelerated.'[5]

13) **Be Fast as Lightning:** Things are changing quickly, and a good leader will be able to keep up. Customer and employee expectations are changing, and executives need to know how to adapt and make informed decisions on the fly. If your organization wants to be prepared for the twenty-first century, you must look at the environment in which your leaders are being produced. Providing them with the tools that will empower, educate and train them is a proactive move that will set your organization apart in the revolution that is coming.

14) **Think Out of the Box:** Get out of your comfort zone and think beyond conventional frameworks. This entails

---

[5]Leon C Megginson, 'Lessons from Europe for American Business', *The Southwestern Social Science Quarterly*, Vol. 44/1, 1963, http://www.jstor.org/stable/42866937.

anticipating changes in your competitive environment, such as the possibility that you are now operating in a different industry than you anticipated, comprehending new market dynamics around competition, determining your new business model, leveraging the experience of different generations and embracing curiosity and diversity.

15) **Know the Power of Influence:** Internal and external stakeholders have greater leverage than ever before. The age of the autocratic boss is over. The power to persuade is now as necessary a skillset for corporate CEOs as much as it is for politicians, because today's generation wants to be collaborated with, not *ruled*. You cannot evoke productivity out of fear as much as you can out of genuine respect and persuasion.

16) **Be a Creator:** Innovate broadly. And I'm not simply referring to product development. It's fine to create new products, but it's only one note on a piano full of potential advances. If your organization is serious about standing out from the crowd, it must constantly innovate across all dimensions: consider new processes and a new business model. After all, your product is only a small component of your overall brand.

17) **Management and Leadership Are Best Friends:** Make management a vital part of your modern leadership. Effective leaders are effective managers. Effective managers are effective leaders.

18) **Be Dynamic:** For better global communication, use a variety of modes and styles, and operate with a global perspective. Speaking many languages, as well as developing sensitivity, empathy, open-mindedness, behaving with respect for others at all times, and having both a readiness to explore and a global sense of curiosity are all steps along this route.

Takeaways

- Twenty-first century leadership is far from traditional business leadership. Be the change, and be it now!
- Global leaders are inclusive, dynamic, adaptable and unafraid of taking risks.
- Today's leaders prioritize their greatest resource—their workers.
- You cannot be a twenty-first century global leader without innovation and creativity.
- Embracing technology and change is the biggest element of being a leader today.

2

THE REMARKABLE LEADER

Leadership is the ability to get extraordinary achievement from ordinary people.

—Brian Tracy

Daniel Goleman argues that a leader has a whopping 70 per cent impact on an organization's climate which, in turn, impacts business performance. One person impacting the organization to such a great extent, could you have imagined? Let's etch this into our heads: leadership runs the gamut—extraordinary, great, good, bad, terrible and just plain awful (you might be familiar with the last three ones, if not the first two, I'm sure.)

Efficient leaders influence a variety of outcomes—including turnover, customer satisfaction, sales, revenue, productivity and more. Effective leadership creates employee engagement and passion, which leads to higher levels of customer loyalty, service, innovation and ultimately, profits.

Judy Marks is the CEO of Otis Elevator and leads a team of over 70,000 employees around the world. According to Judy, leadership is defined as, 'I think it's really the ability to drive results, and I'll leave that word results fairly generic. My role in terms of leadership is to set the vision and to share it. To create an environment where people can resonate not only with the mission but deliver it. To eliminate obstacles so my team can succeed."[6]

Another successful leader, Hans Vestberg, CEO of Verizon Communications, an American multinational telecommunications conglomerate with over 152,000 employees around the world, believes that leadership is: 'Ensuring that people have everything they need to achieve the missions of an organization. That's it. All else is footnotes.'[7]

What definition of leadership do you agree with the most? Do you think there lies a difference between good leadership and *exceptional* leadership? I sure do!

There's a stark contrast between good leaders and bad leaders. It's often easy to point out bad leaders in past organizations or looking in from the outside. However, how do you really differentiate between a good leader and an *exceptionally* good leader?

Great leaders are not just 'better' than good leaders. They are a class apart. They don't just run the game, they *reinvent* and run the game.

When brilliant leadership is in place in a company, it can be felt *throughout* the entire organization. Corporate culture is not imposed but rather developed under this type of leadership. The lines of communication are kept open and are maintained

---

[6] Judy Marks, 'Judy Mark's Post' [LinkedIn Post], https://www.linkedin.com/posts/judy-marks-otis_the-future-leader-9-skills-and-mindsets-activity-6635897178088972288-PGqd, Accessed on 16 March 2022.

[7] Jacob Morgan, '14 Top CEOs Share Their Definition Of "Leadership," What's Yours?', The Future Organization, 13 August 2020, https://thefutureorganization.com/14-top-ceos-share-their-definition-of-leadership%E2%80%8B-whats-yours/, Accessed on 16 March 2022.

on a daily basis. Everyone understands the organization's vision and goals and has suggestions for how they might be enhanced. Employees believe that they are an integral component of the company's overall success and that every task matters. Promotions are decided by selecting people with integrity—whose skills and experience are the most appropriate for the roles. Employees are encouraged to compete with themselves in order to advance, and they recognize that helping their co-workers succeed is the best way for them to advance as well.

First and foremost, exceptional leaders care about their people. They are willing to go the extra mile to serve and get the job done, while simultaneously ensuring the well-being of their employees. They understand that a company isn't really successful if its numbers improve but the people aren't happy.

If you've been lucky enough to have the chance to work for a great leader, you know those lasting feelings: an exceptional leader inspires you to be better, mentors you along the way and gives you the tools to succeed. Exceptional leaders assist others around them in improving—to the point where their subordinates are better equipped than the leader. Individuals that are driven and engaged are more likely to work harder and better, resulting in financial success. Employees that work for such leaders are motivated to come to work and provide their best effort. According to a study by Zenger Folkman, strong leaders may double a company's earnings merely by motivating and engaging employees. High-quality leaders in organizations are 13 times more likely to outperform their competition.

Exceptional leaders produce more extraordinary leaders. You're more likely to develop those skills and abilities if you work for someone you admire and who demonstrates excellent leadership abilities. A great leader is like a pebble dropped in a pond who creates ripples of other good leaders all around them for years to come.

Let's be honest here, goodness is appreciated, but it isn't really *celebrated* in the cut-throat business world. Only *greatness* is. To watch exceptional leaders work can be awe-inspiring. They energize those who work for them, uproot complacency and can shock a failing group or company into success with their personality alone. Good leaders often protect the status quo. They keep a good thing going and improve piecemeal ideas around them. This is obviously a good strategy. A great deal of what they manage to achieve has been through small innovations that have been stacked, one upon the other. Not all of their advancements have come this far, however. There have been those moments in history where one man or woman shaped the very destiny of a country, a field or the world itself. They did not just innovate piecemeal. They changed the very name of the game.

How Do You Spot the Difference Between a Good and an Exceptional Leader?

Good Leaders	*Exceptional Leaders*
A good leader often works towards protecting the current state of affairs. They keep the good ideas going, work around them and witness gradual growth.	The exceptional leader, on the other hand, becomes a game changer. They innovate, generate ideas of their own and make them work.
A good leader builds upon existing knowledge and ideas. Good leaders are able to enhance the status quo. At most, they might push the tiller in another direction and thereby turn the ship slightly.	The exceptional leader disrupts! In today's fast-paced world, only the most innovative survive. Being disruptive takes ingenuity, innovation and the courage to be different.

	Exceptional leaders invent new technologies, new ideas and realize there are vastly new ways to look at things.
	This can make such leaders intimidating for others. After all, many people have a lot to lose when the status quo is endangered. That's why great leaders attract a lot of attention—and it isn't always positive.
A good leader impresses you with their capacity. Leaders who impress you with their capabilities and knowledge are good.	However, the ones who have the ability to make you feel better are considered to be exceptional. The exceptional leader has the ability to impress you with who *you* are. They make you feel good about who you are and what you're capable of.
A good leader only tells you that you're great.	The exceptional leader makes you believe that you're great by showing it. John C. Maxwell says that 'Transformational leaders are belief makers who help people to believe in themselves'[*] and I cannot help but agree.

---

[*]John Maxwell, 'Your Leadership Can Transform the World', Maxwell Leadership, 5 March 2019, https://www.johnmaxwell.com/blog/your-leadership-can-transform-the-world/, Accessed on 17 March 2022.

Good leaders make sure that everyone around is working properly; they ensure efficiency and effectiveness is maintained—but from a distance.	Exceptional leaders, on the other hand, are a part of every single project. They take a personal stake in whatever project they are working on.
A good leader can help people become better at what they're doing.	The exceptional leader can do so much more. They can take a team and make each individual brilliant at what they do by inspiring them to learn and to be the best version of themselves that they can be.
To be a good leader, you needn't look ahead for the long run too much. You can simply motivate those that work for you and depend on them for direction. You're more of a catalyst, rather than somebody that shows/paves the way.	Exceptional leaders, on the other hand, are *both* the catalyst and the rudder. They know where they're going, and they're willing to put in the hard work to get there. They're like Duracell bunnies with an inbuilt compass.
A good leader comes out to be bigger than life, having huge responsibilities, hardcore discipline and a different lifestyle.	On the other hand, you will be able to relate to the exceptional leader. They will be someone you can trust and call your friend. These kinds of leaders do not show the difference between themselves and you. They work towards diminishing the gap between the team and them. They're both your superiors and your allies.

	They are great leaders because they can assert their authority without needing to do so all the time.
Good leaders usually strive for personal growth first and then take the team along with them.	Exceptional leaders elevate the entire team with them at every step. As Jack Welch says, 'Before you are a leader, success is all about growing yourself. When you become a leader, success is all about growing others.'*
A good leader finds solutions to their team's weaknesses.	The exceptional leader turns his and the team's weaknesses into strengths.
A good leader can bark at the rowing team all day long; they can be the most intelligent, capable and talented guide ever. But we would not call this person 'exceptional' if the team isn't growing to be as capable and extraordinary as them.	Exceptional leaders know how to propel a team to greatness. Time after time, what I've seen in business leaders is that the *really* exceptional ones always lead a really great team. They surround themselves with highly capable individuals, and there really isn't any other option.
Good leaders lead the team well. They usually do all of this, *on their own*.	Exceptional leaders, however, create and nurture new leaders to take charge instead of only running the team themselves. Brilliance births brilliance!

---

*Jack Welch, *Winning*, Harper, 2006.

Some people believe that remarkable leadership is implanted in our brains the moment we leave our mothers' wombs—that these leadership skills appear to be encoded as part of our DNA. So, either we're born with the gift of outstanding leadership or we get the short end of the stick. I think that's ridiculous.

There are some experts who believe that extraordinary leaders are not born but rather nurtured and inspired to achieve feats of greatness. And as you've already found out by now, I'm one of them! (Pardon the self-bragging. I'm just trying to channelize an exceptional leader's confidence.)

To lead exceptionally well, one requires a mix of natural and learned abilities that create the ability to adjust in any setting. Given the complexities of a global economy and challenges we've never seen before, succeeding requires extraordinary leaders who are fast as lightning, flexible like a rubber band and nurturing like Mother Teresa—all at the same time.

Now, I know that sounds daunting, but know that *nobody's* born a super-leader (except for a few god-like cases here and there). You can work towards becoming an exceptional leader instead of merely being satisfied with being a good leader.

Exceptional To Extraordinary Leadership

Some traits of exceptional leaders that you can adopt to move closer towards extraordinary leadership:

- **They value their people the most.** An engaged leader sincerely values their people. When you value your people, the culture of your business shifts. People will want to work harder for you and assist you in realizing your business mission. You can have the best offerings, the coolest workplace and the most cutting-edge tools in the world, but if you don't win the hearts and minds of your employees, your company will never be great.

- **They have a bright vision.** What we consider remarkable may, in fact, be the result of intense focus. A bright light can be seen from a long distance, yet it is simply that: light scattered in all directions. Now focus that light with the pinpoint precision of a laser, and that same light can be infinitely more powerful with this intense focus. People that have a personal mission are in the same boat. Those of us who do our best, wherever and whenever we can, can make a significant difference in the world. But those who can operate exclusively within a precise mission rubric are, to borrow the metaphor, laser focused—capable of doing a few truly extraordinary things within the scope of that focus.
- **They don't play superheroes.** In basketball, there is a term called hero ball, where an individual player tries to be the team hero by taking and ultimately missing most of the shots. The problem with hero ball is that the player doesn't involve everyone—which undercuts the team. My favourite boss of all time always figured out a way for us to get in the game because she believed in collaboration. And our team succeeded because we weren't out there missing shots, with a do-it-alone mentality. An optimized team works toward a common goal, complements each other's strengths and offsets each other's weaknesses.
- **They're thick-skinned.** As a leader, you may be subjected to a variety of negative situations, many of which are directed at you. You can't let something like that bring you down as a leader. You must be able to maintain your strength so that you can direct and guide the rest of your crew. You will be a good leader if you can ignore the negativity. You must be able to assume responsibility for a variety of things, even if

they are not your fault, in addition to being thick-skinned. You can't point the finger at others or seek out scapegoats. Accept responsibility for the issue and work to resolve it.
- **They are trendsetters.** Great leaders need to be able to think out of the box—which means they have to be creative thinkers. When you have a creative imagination, you can come up with more innovations and abstract solutions to problems. Leaders are faced with so many problems on a daily basis, and some can only be solved with creativity.
- **They gain power through influence rather than position.** He understands that the respect he receives as a result of his position is temporary. Being the chairman of a committee or the president of another, being a governor or a barrister—all of these positions are temporary. Positions change over time. However, he receives true respect for being a nice guy—for his values and attitude. It lasts a long time.
- **They know their staff *really* well.** To be a great leader, you must assist your employees in honing their skills and realizing their full potential. This necessitates learning about them and their strengths. Consider what your staff excel at. How can you help them grow? Look for opportunities that will open doors and develop their talents.
- **They embrace interdependence.** Jim McCann, one of the early and most successful pioneers of e-commerce and the founder of 1-800-Flowers, sat for an interview with me which was one of my favourite interviews so far. Jim can boast about his individual achievements, but he'll be the first to admit that he would have been a complete failure if he hadn't realized how his fate was always linked to others around him. He realized from an early age that the only way he could achieve the truly extraordinary was to work with synergistically with people in an ecosystem he valued

and utilized to its full potential. Jim's ecosystem consisted of his employees, customers, suppliers, community and even the media.

- **They are extremely competent.** Extraordinary leaders are extraordinarily competent at their craft. The first example that comes to mind is Bill Gates, founder and former chairman of Microsoft. Did you know that Bill Gates has been coding since middle school? He used to sneak out in the middle of the night to a university that was walking distance from his house and offered him complete access to the most cutting-edge computer technology available at the time. Did I mention he used to get spare parts from Bill Hewlett—of Hewlett-Packard? That's like being an aspiring fashion designer and living next door to Giorgio Armani. At age 13, Gates was playing with cutting-edge computer components like they were Hot Wheels cars or a Happy Meal. Basically, this implies their skilful gaining of knowledge and finding almost any way to put that knowledge to good use.
- **They go beyond their comfort zones.** Anything creative and dynamic can happen only when you stretch yourself beyond your comfort zone. You are often stuck here. You may think that you cannot do something. But if you make an effort and take that first step, you will find that you are not bound by your comfort zone. A good leader knows this.
- **Bravery is their selling point.** Great leaders can't be afraid of anything. Most importantly, they can't be afraid of failure or taking risks. Leaders often have to take risks in order to get ahead, and that is a good thing. You can't be afraid of failing, because you will be a lot less likely to take risks. But then, you will most likely stay stagnant. If you let go of that fear of failure, you'll be able to get ahead and not be afraid to go out on a limb.

- **They respect themselves, but don't take themselves too seriously.** Being an extraordinary leader isn't easy. It's stressful when all of the key decisions rest on your shoulders. However, a good sense of humour and laughter are contagious mood boosters. People will smile back, laugh along with you and generally have an improved outlook—even in the worst of times.
- **They connect with others, within and beyond their organization.** A true leader creates connections—not just between themselves and the people on their team but between the team members themselves; and also between their team and their customers. You have to set the example that building strong connections is a part of your culture and your company. Carve out time to connect with your employees and get to know who they are. Being in your own little bubble at the top of your throne will only throw you off it pretty soon.

Takeaways

- The good leader produces results; the exceptional leader transforms the entire organization in the long run.
- The good leader stands out from the team; the exceptional leader blends in and leads by setting an example.
- The good leader has personal ambitions; the exceptional leader dreams big even for their employees.
- Exceptional leaders break status-quo; they innovate and break away from conventions and standards—both at the workplace and beyond it. That's what makes them so powerful.

3

STYLE YOUR OWN LEADERSHIP

The best leaders don't know just one style of leadership—they're skilled at several, and have the flexibility to switch between styles as the circumstances dictate.[8]

—Daniel Goleman

'A good leader should always…'

How did you mentally complete that sentence? Pay attention to that, because it has *a lot* to do with your customized leadership style and methods. It's almost like knowing your favourite ice-cream flavour or knowing what genre of films makes you the happiest on a rainy weekend—just a tad bit more complex, of course!

Leadership is a fluid practise. We're always changing and improving the way in which we help our direct reports and the company grow. And the longer we lead, the more likely we'll change the way we choose to complete the sentence above.

I can vouch for the fact that, at some point in your career,

---

[8]Daniel Goleman, 'Leadership That Gets Results', *Harvard Business Review*, March 2000, https://hbr.org/2000/03/leadership-that-gets-results, Accessed on 17 March 2022.

you will take on a leadership role in some capacity (especially after becoming a great workplace leader, because you're reading this book).

Whether you're leading a meeting, a project, a team or an entire department, you might consider identifying with or adopting a defined leadership style. 'Identifying our leadership style is important because it gives us insight into other people's experience of us,' noted Clare Monteau, PhD, an organizational scientist. 'We can't possibly know other people's experience of the world. And that can lead to many misunderstandings and opportunities for miscommunication that damage our ability to lead effectively and powerfully.'

Most professionals develop their own style of leadership based on factors like experience and personality—as well as the unique needs of their company and its organizational culture. This chapter tells you how to weave your own leadership style and *own* it.

But you might want to ask: why exactly do you *need* a leadership style?

As you gain experience as a leader, you'll likely use a variety of processes and strategies to satisfy your employer's goals and the needs of the people who report to you. You may use a variety of leadership styles as a leader-manager at any one time to be effective. You don't have to wait until you are in the C-suite to start honing your personal leadership style. You can build the essential habit of self-awareness no matter where you are in your work.

Everyone's approach to finding a style will be different, but there are a few important steps you can take to ensure you're developing a unique approach. Knowing your leadership style is critical because it can help you determine how you affect those whom are under your direct influence. How do the people who directly reports to you see you? Do they feel you're an effective leader?

A group of researchers led by psychologist Kurt Lewin set out in 1939 to uncover various leadership styles. In Lewin's experiment, students were divided into three groups, each led by an authoritarian, democratic or delegative leader. The children were then taken through an arts-and-crafts project while researchers observed their behaviour in response to various leadership styles.[9]

Daniel Goleman's 'Six Leadership Styles' is another foundational study on leadership styles. Goleman is most recognized for his work on Emotional Intelligence, but he also conducted a ground-breaking study on leadership, 'Leadership that Gets Results,' which was published in the *Harvard Business Review* in 2000.

You can save yourself the trouble of going through these studies, because I've combined some of the dominant leadership styles prevalent in the business world today. See where you fit, or if you don't fit at all (I'll explain why that can be beneficial to you. Exceptional leaders don't remain limited to a single category or approach, remember?)

---

[9] Kurt Lewin, 'Patterns of aggressive behavior in experimentally created social climates', *Journal of Social Psychology*, May 1939, Vol. 10/2, Pp. 271, https://doi.org/10.1080/00224545.1939.9713366.

Type	Meaning	Example
The Autocrat—'Do as I tell you!'	Also called 'the authoritarian style of leadership,' this type of leader is focused almost entirely on results and efficiency. The autocrat often makes decisions alone or with a small, trusted group and expects employees to do exactly what they're asked. It can be helpful to think of these types of leaders as military commanders. While results are fast in this kind of leadership, employees may not be content.	Before an operation, the surgeon carefully recounts the rules and processes of the operation room with every team member who will be helping during the surgery. They want to ensure everyone is clear on the expectations and follows each procedure carefully and exactly so that the surgery goes as smoothly as possible.
The Democrat—'What do you think about this?'	Lewin's study found that participative leadership, also known as democratic leadership, is typically the most effective leadership style. Such leaders show high levels of teamwork, emotional intelligence and brilliant communication skills.	As a store manager, Tommy has hired many brilliant and focused team members who he trusts. When deciding on storefronts and floor design, Tommy acts only as the final moderator for his team to move forward with their ideas.

	This type of leadership is effective at fostering ownership in a project, but it might result in delayed progress toward objectives until a certain amount of momentum has been established. Anyone who wants to employ this method must ensure that senior managers are on board with the procedure and recognize that reaching consensus may take some time.	He is there to answer questions and present possible improvements for his team to consider.
The Coach— 'Try this… let me show you.'	When you have a coaching leadership style, you tend to have a 'consider this' approach. A leader, who coaches, views people as a reservoir of talent to be developed. The leader who takes a coach approach aims to help people reach their full potential.	Sales Manager Tyler gathers his team of account executives for a meeting to discuss learnings from the previous quarter. They begin the meeting by completing a collective assessment of the team's strengths, weaknesses, opportunities and threats.

	Leaders that employ a coaching style open their hearts and doors to others. They believe that everyone possesses personal power. A coaching leader provides people with some guidance in order to help them reach their maximum potential.	The manager then honours specific team members for outstanding work and reviews the team's accomplishments. Finally, the manager concludes the meeting by announcing a contest that will begin the next quarter in order to encourage salespeople to fulfil their targets.
The Hands-Off Leader— 'It's your task. Handle it your way.'	This is the polar opposite of autocratic leadership, which focuses on delegating a large number of responsibilities to team members while providing little to no monitoring. Laissez-faire leaders have more time to devote to other tasks, because they do not spend their time extensively managing employees.	When welcoming new employees, Maria explains that her engineers are free to set and maintain their own work schedules— as long as they are working toward and achieving team goals. They are also free to learn about and engage in projects outside of their team that they are interested in.

	When all team members are highly experienced, well-trained and require little oversight, managers may use this leadership style. However, if employees are unsure of their boss's expectations, or if some team members require regular motivation and boundaries to work properly, productivity may suffer.	
The Pace-Setter—'Do as I do, now!'	'Keep up!' can be another phrase most indicative of leaders who utilize the pacesetting style. As in racing, this style depicts a highly motivated leader who sets the pace. Pacesetters raise the bar and encourage their teammates to sprint to the finish line.	The leader of a weekly meeting realized that taking an hour out of everyone's schedule once a week wasn't enough to justify the meeting's objective. She altered the meeting to a 15-minute stand-up with only those she had updates for to boost efficiency.

The Visionary—'How about something new?'	By inspiring colleagues and garnering trust for fresh ideas, visionary leaders may propel growth and usher in moments of transition. A visionary leader can also establish a strong organizational tie. They work hard to instil trust in both direct reporters and co-workers.	A teacher creates a group at work for colleagues who want to help resolve anxieties and issues students have outside of school. The goal is to help students better focus on and succeed at school. He has developed testing methods so that they can find meaningful ways to help students in a quick and efficient way.
The Servant—'People come first.'	Such leaders demonstrate empathy, and strong communication skills and are very good at building relationships. When a team has gone through a tough experience and needs to mend rifts or generate motivation, this technique is most effective. Because it is not a very goal-oriented style, anyone who employs it must ensure that others understand that the purpose is team cohesion rather than specific tasks.	A product manager hosts monthly one-on-one coffee meetings with everyone who has concerns, questions or thoughts about improving or using the product. This time is meant for her to address the needs of and help those who are using the product in any capacity.

Found yourself fitting into any of these? If not, don't worry. You can customize your distinct leadership style the way you customize your dressing style, speaking style and your lifestyle. 'Humans don't fit into neat little boxes,' said Michelle Duval, business coach and CEO of Fingerprint for Success, an online coaching start-up. 'Looking at motivations and attitudes takes into account the fact that people adapt and mature. It allows for a much more dynamic view of humans and how their leadership styles can change over time.'[10]

Tips on Finding Your Leadership Style

1) **Mimicry Is Foolish:** Before you move into your first management position, you may have assumptions of what a leader should look, sound and act like. Steve Jobs and Sheryl Sandberg's leadership styles are not for everyone. In truth, no two leadership approaches are alike. Throw that archetype out the window when you discover yourself imitating your idol's style. The job of building your unique style does not begin outside of yourself; rather, it begins within. If you aren't loyal to yourself, following a leadership style that doesn't suit you will drain you of your energy.

2) **Know Thyself:** Consider the characteristics that come easily to you. Then ask yourself, 'Where do you have difficulty?' You may be a quick learner who excels at getting things done, but you occasionally trade quality for quantity. Alternatively, you may feel secure in the work you produce on your own but find it difficult to speak up about your

---

[10]Catherine Tansey, 'How to Identify Your Leadership Style', Lattice, 8 January 2021, https://lattice.com/library/how-to-identify-your-leadership-style, Accessed on 17 March 2021.

contributions in a meeting. When you initially take on a leadership role, the habits you develop as an individual contributor may become your default. However, becoming a great manager necessitates self-improvement in order to help and grow others—which requires a different type of effort. It's crucial to be honest with yourself about your strengths and weaknesses.

Here's a little table for you to know your leadership preferences a tad bit better:

	Just like me! (3 points)	*A lot like me. (2 points)*	*A little bit like me. (1 point)*	*Not at all like me. (0 points)*	Total Score:
1) I believe teams work best when everyone is involved in taking decisions.					
2) I can see situations from many different perspectives.					
3) I can take on a leadership role when needed but don't consider myself a 'leader'.					
4) I'm good at bringing out the best in other people.					
5) I'm happy to act as the spokesperson for our group.					
6) I think the most important thing for a group is the wellbeing of its members.					
7) I don't mind how long discussions last, so long as we consider every angle.					
8) I set myself high standards and expect others to do the same for themselves.					

9) I am good at organizing other people.					
10) I enjoy working in committees. Teamwork excites me.					
11) I think all group members should abide by formal decisions, so long as we follow proper procedures.					
12) I'm good at adapting to different situations. I embrace change and do not have a rigid personality.					
13) I'm determined to push projects forward and get results.					
14) I love helping other people to develop.					
15) I think people should be allowed to make mistakes in order to learn.					
16) I enjoy role-playing exercises.					

Now, add the total for the following combination of questions (this will end soon, I promise!)

Question Combinations	Added Points	Preferred Leadership Style
4, 8, 6, 9		Facilitative/Servant
2, 3, 12, 16		Situational
1, 7, 10, 11		Democratic
5, 8, 9, 13		Authoritative/Autocratic

Whichever category has the highest added points, is somewhat your natural leadership style.

3) **Next, Identify What You Want:** Identifying your leadership style isn't simply a result of being told, 'This is how you are,' after taking an assessment. Rather, individuals can take an active role in shaping their leadership style by reflecting on the characteristics and skills they've admired in other leaders and working to embody those traits. We don't exist—or work—in a vacuum. Valuable information can be learned from observing what the leaders around you are doing well and then adopting those same characteristics in your interactions—but with your *own* twist.

4) **Ask Your Team for Advice:** As a leader, it can feel vulnerable to seek out and receive this kind of feedback. But outside input helps contextualize the other information you have about your leadership style. Again, leadership doesn't happen in a vacuum, and how the people you are leading perceive you is a crucial piece of the puzzle.

5) **Practise Your Natural Style:** Build on your default leadership style. Practise the new behaviours until they become natural. In other words, don't use a different leadership style as a 'point-and-click' approach. People can smell a fake leadership style from *miles* away—authenticity rules.

6) **Rely on Others:** Keep track of whom on your team possess the abilities and personalities that you find particularly challenging, and encourage them to take the lead when their approach is more suited than yours. Do you have a hard time forming ties and maintaining team harmony, but you've noticed that Ella, one of your co-workers, constantly manages to make things better? When the scenario calls for affiliative leadership, use that skill: step back and let Ella lead. After all, the finest leaders are those who develop other leaders, not those who follow them.

7) **Lastly, Adapt To (Survive) Thrive:** Traditional leadership

styles are still relevant in today's workplace, but they may need to be combined with new approaches in line with how leadership is defined for the twenty-first century. Because of changing demographics and various employee demands, today's business environments are plagued with difficulties. This may require the emergence of a new type of leader—one who combines many of the leadership styles outlined here. Continue reading to learn more about this in the next chapter. Are you all set?

Takeaways

- You have to change your leadership style according to situations and employees' personalities.
- You do have a natural leadership style, even if you cannot see it right now.
- Understand your natural leadership style and your personality, and then create goals to achieve your ideal leadership style.
- Do not mimic other leaders; create your own statement that's authentic and raw.
- There's no one fixed definition of leadership. Your leadership style, however stable, should be malleable and dynamic. The twenty-first century leader adapts to thrive, remember?

4

ADAPT TO (SURVIVE) THRIVE

The most important factor in survival is neither intelligence nor strength but adaptability.

—Charles Darwin

How do you prepare yourself mentally to handle whatever life throws at you when you wake each morning? Do you end up feeling anxious and worried when you think about what each day holds for you?

Kenneth Blanchard, author of *The One Minute Manager*, states that '54 per cent of leaders use only one leadership style, regardless of the situation, which means that 50 per cent of the time, leaders are using the wrong leadership style to meet the needs of their people.'[11] That way, they're unable to tap the maximum potential of an employee or keep their employees content.

Change is inevitable in life and, naturally, at work. We've already learnt that the hard way—thanks to the pandemic. Leaders who adapt easily are the ones not only surviving but thriving in business and organizations.

---

[11] Kenneth Blanchard, *The One Minute Manager*, HarperCollins, 2006.

Any great leader knows there are a lot of variables to consider when you work with a team. Each member of the team has their own:

- Background
- Learning/working style
- Personality
- Motivators
- Experiences
- Preferences
- Skill sets and strengths
- Weaknesses

No team is perfect. How then do you, as a leader, adapt your leadership style according to different team members to maximize their outputs? This is where adaptive, situational leadership comes to the rescue.

Leaders, all over the world, are facing constant change and complexity—including new cultures, new jobs, new markets and new competition. To thrive as a leader requires the ability to adapt to these changes and adjust to the new conditions and different personalities.

The premise of situational leadership theory is that there is no one-size-fits-all approach to leadership. Rather than the permanent talents or traits of the leader, what counts as the most effective leadership style varies on the situation of an organization—what tasks or challenges are at hand. The situational leader assesses their team or organization by simply inquiring about the current state of affairs. They do what is required to successfully lead the team based on the understanding gained by answering this question. Why limit yourself to a single style when you can have them all?

If you want to succeed as a leader, you can't afford to be

inflexible. Adaptable leaders earn the respect of their colleagues and motivate those they lead to embrace change—making business operation as smooth as possible.

In an article titled, 'Why Flexible and Adaptive Leadership Is Essential' Rubina Mahsud and Gary Yukl suggest, 'Threats which are often unanticipated will always arise to sink an organization, damage properties, and lives. One way an organization can survive this threat is by responding quickly to these threats when they arise. Adaptive leadership is what every organization need if they are to survive troubling times.'[12] Now, more than ever before, leaders all over the world are facing change and complexity—the coronavirus pandemic has presented us all with new challenges, new circumstances and new uncertainties. Jobs have been morphing, expanding, shrinking and disappearing. Co-workers, teammates and technology are changing rapidly. According to Paul Hersey and Kenneth Blanchard, 'Effective leaders need to be flexible, and must adapt themselves according to the situation.'

Here's What Adapting to Change for Successful Executives Means

- Adapt to the changing external pressures facing the organization.
- Adjust their management style to changing situations and employees.
- Accept changes as positive.
- Revise plans as necessary.
- Consider other people's concerns during change.

---

[12] Gary Yukl and Rubina Mahsud, 'Why flexible and adaptive leadership is essential', *Consulting Psychology Journal: Practise and Research*, Vol. 62/2, Pp. 81–93, 2010, https://doi.org/10.1037/a0019835.

Situational Leadership is a highly adaptive and dynamic leadership style. This technique encourages leaders to assess their teams, consider the multiple variables at work, and select the leadership style that best suits their objectives and circumstances. In the past, a leader was a boss. Today's leaders cannot lead merely on the basis of their positional authority.

Situational leaders evaluate the situation, the circumstances and the individuals involved in their approach. Then, they choose the most *appropriate* type of leadership style to use for that given circumstance and employee. Instead of being locked into one general leadership style, all of them are incorporated into their approach, which makes them so powerful.

Did you have a boss that took the time to explain things to you, guide you and assist you in your job? This form of coaching management style could have been crucial to your achievement and professional progress when you didn't have much expertise. Let's fast forward to a later stage in your career. You now have the knowledge, skills and expertise to easily fulfil your role and achieve your objectives. You value a management who takes a more hands-off approach in this situation—one who gives you the freedom to make your own choices. Different management approaches are required for different degrees of skill. Different situations, personalities and tasks can all do this. A manager may let a high-performing employee to oversee their own project. In contrast, a high-profile project or a crisis might dictate that a manager gets more involved.

- It's highly flexible.
- It's easy to adapt depending on the scenario.
- It's straightforward and intuitive.
- It accounts for many different working styles and personalities.

- It boosts collaboration, communication, productivity and morale in teams.
- It encourages leaders to be transparent about goals.
- It encourages leaders to be creative.
- It allows leaders to nurture the development of their subordinates.
- It accounts for challenges and unforeseen obstacles.
- It focuses on relationship-building.
- It enables the leader to better control outcomes.

Why Is Situational Leadership So Effective in the Modern World?

One of the keys to situational leadership is adaptability. To satisfy the changing needs of a business and its people, leaders must be able to switch between leadership styles. These leaders must be able to recognize when to modify their management style and what leadership strategy is best for each new paradigm. To be a good situational leader, you must possess the following characteristics:

1) **Flexibility:** A situational leader pays close attention to the changing needs of the team, task and organization. They adjust their leadership style as needed to bring out the best in team members and ensure successful outcomes.

    They can simultaneously hold multiple scenarios in mind and can see when to shift and inject a change.

    Leaders with situational flexibility also vary their approach to dealing with their own and others' emotions—an area that many leaders often fail to consider. An emotionally flexible leader is comfortable with the process of transitioning, including grieving, complaining and resistance.

2) **Observing and Listening:** Active listening. To understand what's going on and meet their team's needs, a situational leader must leverage their active listening skills.
3) **Guts:** It takes a lot of courage for a leader to try out different leadership approaches and figure out which one is ideal. Most leaders stick to a particular way of doing things—whatever has worked best for them in the past. A situational leader is not afraid to take chances and to adopt a radically different leadership style if the situation demands it.
4) **Coaching Skills:** Situational leaders must improve their abilities to coach at a variety of developmental levels in order to be most effective. This ability enables them to meet teammates where they are and assist them in getting to where they need to be.
5) **Integrity:** Situational leaders prioritize the sustainability of their organization and encourage their followers without manipulating the situation at hand. Situational leaders are not motivated by a desire to unfairly capitalize on the weaknesses of their team or organization. A leader that might be a strong pacesetter will have to make sure that their followers do not experience burnout and *know* when to listen to their needs.

Be a Chameleon

Do you feel like things aren't getting done in your workplace? Maybe your team has stopped achieving targets, or milestones are being missed while your costs are still high as a kite? Though it may be tempting to lay the blame at the feet of your team, an intuitive, situational leader will look inward first. Perhaps your leadership style is not right for the situation or for a particular employee. Perhaps, it never has been? Here's when dynamic leadership comes in—full-force.

Case I: Show and Tell

Mary's best quality (and the *only* good quality, honestly) as a worker, is that she's present in the workplace. She never causes any issues. However, she never innovates or contributes to projects either. You constantly have to ask her if the work has been done and more frequently, why it hasn't been completed yet.

Mary is quiet, and the good thing is, she never complains about her firm, boss or co-workers; but honestly, it's as though she's not there in the office. She stays mum during meetings, she nods her head robotically when you give her a task, and talking with her is like playing tennis against a wall—you're the only one putting in work. Although Mary isn't problematic, neither is she productive. And yet, she's obviously eating into your company's budget, without giving much in return. What a crisis.

This is where you *tell* or *direct*. You have no choice but to engage Mary through micro-management and by telling her *what* you *exactly* want and *when* you want it. With this style of leadership, Mary does exactly what she is told, because honestly, she takes no decisions herself and isn't driven to take any either.

People who don't have the right knowledge or skills for the role/job and also lack the willingness to finish tasks, need a little bit of authoritative commands. After all, you got to get your work done, right?

Case II: Play the Coach

Max is undoubtedly one of the strongest performers of your team; he turns up to work on time, energetic and regular. There's this fire in his eyes and you see it. Max's dedication and willingness to work is what actually impressed you the most about him during the interview. He has great commitment and does tasks within deadlines, delivering quality results exactly *how* you wanted them to be delivered.

However, Max requires the most of your time and energy. He may have the drive, but he isn't exactly proactive and constantly needs guidance with tasks. You wish he'd take the initiative to make things happen and trust his own judgement. He's always outside your room waiting to tell you about new problems he's facing or how he's stuck at the project you'd given him a few days ago.

People who are willing to finish the tasks—but who don't have the knowledge, confidence or skills required to do so—require your supervision. Like Max, these are developing team members who may not yet have the specific skill set required for a task, but they have a high level of commitment. In such cases, you *coach*, i.e., you provide guidance.

Since Max's maturity is still low, but the willingness is there. Your job, as a leader, is to help teammates like Max gain experience and confidence. Tap his energy, coach him and help him gain experience until he doesn't have to stand outside your door for constant approval and validation; saves you time and energy and nurtures the potential leader in him.

Case III: All Polly Needs Is a Little Push

Polly's résumé is shiny. After all, you hired her after interviewing almost 34 candidates. Being a Post-Graduate from an Ivy League University, she projected an impressive intelligence and skill set that *you* wish you had when you were her age.

Also, you loved the way she conducted herself—professional, soft-spoken and the best thing was that she knew exactly what knowledge the job position required her to possess, and she fit those requirements like a hand fitting a velvet glove.

However, you saw one red flag—a lack in confidence and drive. *Ironical*, you thought. How could someone from an Ivy League look like she was slightly jittery and intimidated? You told yourself it could be due to her being new to your firm, but over time, you realized this was a recurring issue.

People like Polly, who have the right knowledge or skills for the role/job but who lack the willingness to take responsibility and/or finish the tasks due to a lack of confidence or motivation, need you to *support* and *participate* with them. These developed team members are *highly* skilled and may, sometimes, have even more expertise than *you* (I know it's hard to swallow), but they may showcase a lack of drive or confidence in performing a particular task.

What do you do? You appeal to their emotions. All they need is a push to realize who they are. Remind them *why* you selected them and why they have no reason to feel underconfident. If their lack of drive comes from a burnout, ask them ways you can help them with their tasks or issues.

Tap into their desire for impact and sense of meaning or purpose—basically, ask them what motivates them, what they're looking to get through this job, and last of all, tell them you trust them. Give them inputs and suggestions, but let *them* make the final decisions. That way, they feel powerful, feel in-control and feel a sense of value that drives them to be engaged at work. This automatically enhances their confidence.

All Polly needs is support, not your coaching; she already possesses the best of skills needed for her position, remember?

Case IV: Share the Burden

When you'd first hired John, you didn't realize he would become *very* important to your firm. He was obviously impressive and confident, but he didn't exactly strike you as a star performer *until* he actually began working under you. Thank God for John.

Switch to the present, and losing John is a dreadful nightmare for you. He's an absolute joy to work with, and it's because of him you achieve your goals without ripping your hair apart. John completes his tasks flawlessly, without causing any office politics or arguments. Rather, he solves problems and interpersonal conflicts like a boss.

You often wonder what you would do if he decided to leave your team? You're sure he has so many options since he's both skilled and driven—basically, an absolute powerhouse. His résumé screams experience and expertise, and so does his work and personality.

Apart from this, he's not arrogant, delivers quality results on time and leads the team almost as well as you (slightly intimidating, right? Understandable.)

A team member like John, can perform a task at a sustained and acceptable level, and is both confident and motivated to do so. These developed team members are highly skilled—often more so than their leader themselves—and they have a high level of motivation and commitment. What do you do with a man like John? You *delegate*. You empower him to work independently towards achieving agreed-upon goals, not only because you trust him with his work so much but also because you want to foster the leader in him and make him feel important and relied upon. That way, John remains content in your organization and also shares your burden. Of course, you provide feedback every now and then and talk to John about important decisions, but you let John have his way with *how* tasks are achieved. You save time and energy, and John finds the leader and decision-maker within him. A perfect win-win situation.

Here Are the Kinds of Leaders You Do Not Want to Be

After all, bad leaders can be like a cancer to a company or the workplace, making even the most loyal and skilled employees leave. The sad part is that many workers like the company they work for and their job role. They just can't stand their leader—the person with which they likely have the most contact. If you don't want to drive your team away at the speed of lightning, avoid being:

1) **The Invisible Leader:** The most common kind of incompetent leader isn't the ranting, narcissistic sociopath that might immediately come to your mind when you think of powerful people at the workplace. Rather, it's the invisible leader—the one in power, who is psychologically absent and detached from their role and team. The worst part is, this leader continues to enjoy the privileges and rewards of a leadership role but avoids meaningful involvement with their team.

    Research shows that being ignored by one's boss is more alienating than being treated poorly. Invisible leaders specialize in flying under the radar by not doing anything that attracts attention. However, the damages caused by them aren't really invisible. Look out for them, and of course, don't be one of them.

2) **The People-Pleaser:** Bossy bosses are easy to spot and quickly become unbearable. The leader who lacks authority—with other leaders, employees, clients, consumers and so on—is often less obvious.

    These leaders, on the other hand, have the potential to be just as awful. They avoid making difficult decisions, fail to make necessary changes, and provide unsatisfactory feedback.

The people-pleasing leader is preoccupied with relationships and how to keep them from being ruined. They have a great demeanour, but they find uncomfortable conversations (such as performance assessments) very difficult and will usually simply tell you what you want to hear—even if you have areas where you can improve.

While there's nothing wrong with fostering an environment where people feel appreciated, validated and happy, when you're too concerned about being everyone's best friend, you only fail your employees. Consider it this way: as much as parents want to spoil their children, they also recognize that part of the deal is shaping the child into a person who will one day be responsible, successful and upstanding—and that sometimes means making difficult decisions, setting firmer expectations or pushing your team beyond their comfort zone. The same rule applies to leadership.

3) **The Narcissist:** Now this is a category we're the *most* familiar with, aren't we?

    Narcissistic bosses always look out for being on top. They are less concerned about the happiness of the people who directly reports to them and more focused on what's in it for *them*. Instead of coaching, leading and supporting, they like to boss people around and take credit for their achievements. Narcissists may steal sales leads away from their team members or take all of the glory for a big project that was a group effort. Basically, it's always me, myself and I.

4) **The Control-Freak:** These leaders lead in micromanaging others and are obsessed with 'musts'. At work, they are dedicated, yet their demand for control causes them to be rigid and inflexible. They're always frightened of making a mistake. It's a minefield working with controllers. You never

know when you'll have to pay a high emotional price for breaking some unspoken, yet unbreakable rule.
5) **The Parasite:** Again, another category that makes all of us shudder. Parasites suck the life out of you; they don't respect work-life balance.

    They email, call or text their employees at all hours of the day with no sense of boundary. They tend to work well into the evening, often firing off urgent emails to their team at 2 am. They basically have a 'nose to the grindstone' mentality with zero affinity for workplace culture, bonding or happiness. These are the kinds of bad leaders who will cancel a team birthday lunch or call their workers during their vacation.

Takeaways

- Situational leadership is very effective, because it makes the most out of various situations and different personalities.
- Situational leaders know their employees inside out, not just professionally but also personally.
- To be a situational leader, your key activity is to observe and listen to your employees, their needs, their motivators and their weaknesses.
- The situational leader takes risks, because it's always a leap of faith to use different leadership styles in different circumstances.
- To be an exceptional leader, you must first know the leadership styles you need to avoid: the narcissist, the micromanager, the one who's never there, the one who doesn't respect boundaries and the one who pleases employees a little too much.

5

TWO SIDES OF THE SAME COIN: MANAGEMENT AND LEADERSHIP

Management is efficiency in climbing the ladder of success; leadership determines whether the ladder is leaning against the right wall.[13]

—Stephen Covey, businessman, keynote speaker and author

The terms 'management' and 'leadership' are frequently used interchangeably. While there is a lot of overlap between what leaders and managers do, there are also a lot of contrasts.

Is it true that a good manager is also a good leader? What is the difference between management and leadership? Leadership and management are frequently thought to have overlapping responsibilities. While this is true, the meanings of these two phrases are distinct and should not be used interchangeably. Both denote a unique collection of functions, qualities and skills with some similarity.

The major distinction between leaders and managers is that leaders have followers, whilst managers have employees. There are several significant differences between being a manager and being a leader.

---

[13]Stephen R. Covey, *The 7 Habits of Highly Effective People,* Free Press, 2004.

Manager	Leader
Achieving set goals: Managers work to achieve corporate goals by adopting processes like budgeting, organizational structuring and personnel. Leaders, on the other hand, are more focused on thinking ahead and seizing chances. It's the process of collaborating with others to guarantee the successful completion of a set of objectives.	**Envisioning new goals:** Leaders are visioners. The majority of them have a clear idea of where they want their companies to go in the future. They are not, however, the only ones who are responsible for bringing that vision to life. Leadership is about developing what the goals should be. It's more about driving change, and it needs management to facilitate change.
Mission: Management spends a good deal of their time focusing on the specific mission of their organization and their team. They need to know the detailed goals for the project's success and help the team come up with a way to reach their goals. A manager's focus on mission helps the team members understand what is expected of them.	**Vision:** Vision is a quality of leadership that entails looking at the big picture. Leaders assist their teams in comprehending the larger role they can perform in assisting the corporation. They inspire the people they work with to share their ideas. They assist teams in seeing their contributions as part of a larger vision for success. They concentrate on some of the larger-scale results and assist everyone in getting on board.

Organization: Managers pursue goals through coordinated actions and tactical processes, or tasks and activities that unfold over stages to reach a certain outcome. For example, they may implement a decision-making process when leading a critical meeting or when devising a plan for communicating organizational change.	**Influence:** Leaders, on the other hand, are more concerned with how to align and influence people rather than how to organize them to get work done. In a leadership position, the primary responsibility is to mobilize others to complete a set of individual and communal duties.
Define Structure: Managers must be well-organized in order to assist their employees in achieving their goals. Project management, meetings, strategy and teamwork are all essential for managers to help their employees feel safe. Managers must devote time to concentrating on particular techniques to be organized in both everyday chores and larger projects. Whatever great idea emerges, managers break it down into smaller tasks and projects that the team can handle.	**Flexible Creativity:** Leadership spends time focused on innovation and devising new and creative strategies. In order for leaders to be effective innovators, they must be creative. They are constantly on the lookout for fresh strategies to assist the organization. Managers may take advantage of both of these acts by seeking for creative ideas that are exciting for their team and assisting in the planning of strategies to bring such ideas to light.

Action: A managerial culture emphasizes rationality and control. In other words, managers always look for answers to 'how and when'. Hence, the manager's main responsibility is to fulfil their tasks based on the leader's vision. Their main job is to ensure that people on different functions with different responsibilities operate efficiently, productively and that they feel like they can share their voice.	**Ideas:** Leaders are more about looking for opportunities for improvement on the organizational level. They do so by coming up with new ideas and driving the shift to a forward-thinking mindset. Leaders can play a critical role in fostering change within organizations, because they are continually looking for fresh ideas. Furthermore, by empowering employees to strive toward common goals, a leader drives constructive, incremental change. Effective communication is a leader's most powerful weapon for doing so.
Drivers of change: Managers are accountable for ensuring their employees' long-term success and a positive work environment throughout their careers. Managers are held accountable for the success and productivity of their teams because they account for over 70 per cent of employee engagement in the workplace.	**Initiators of change:** There is nothing that managers can do to assist their employees succeed if they are not enthused by what their leaders have to say. Leaders may empower their workforce, gain their followers' attention and motivate them to undertake significant organizational projects by creating a personal leadership style through self-reflection, real communication and regular feedback.

A position:	A quality:
The title 'manager' often denotes a specific role within an organization's hierarchy, while referring to someone as a 'leader' has a more fluid meaning. 'Manager is a title. It's a role and set of responsibilities,' says leadership coach Doc Norton in *Forbes*. 'Having the position of manager does not make you a leader. The best managers are leaders, but the two are not synonymous. Leadership is the result of action. If you act in a way that inspires, encourages or engages others, you are a leader. It doesn't matter your title or position.'*	Leadership is a skill that must be honed through time. Professionals of all levels may improve their self-awareness and understanding of how to bring out the best in themselves and others by developing emotional intelligence and learning how to influence others.

---

*Forbes Coaches Council, 'What Makes A Good Leader? Key Differences Between Management And Leadership', *Forbes*, 20 November 2017, https://www.forbes.com/sites/forbescoachescouncil/2017/11/20/what-makes-a-good-leader-key-differences-between-management-and-leadership/?sh=a387892daf5a, Accessed on 22 March 2022.

Present: One of the most significant differences between leaders and managers is that managers are more present-oriented. As a result, the manager's most significant task is to achieve organizational goals by implementing budgeting, organizational structuring and staffing processes and procedures.	**Future:** On the other hand, leaders tend to think ahead and capitalize on future opportunities. Leaders look ahead and create new visions for the organization's future.
Live by Culture: Managers lead their employees to live up to the organizational culture. Culture is a system of values, beliefs and behaviours that shape and determine how an organization operates and how the work gets done. Without collaboration between leadership and management, it is impossible to motivate people to live by the company's culture and basic principles.	**Shape Culture:** Leaders establish and influence organizational culture. It is the leader's responsibility to support the organization's core company values and beliefs by their actions, authentic communication and decisions. Passionate and inspiring leaders have tremendous power to influence employee behaviour and communicate the organizational culture throughout the company.

When Leadership and Management Meet

You've likely had a manager or two in your career that you weren't very fond of. And on the flip side, you've probably worked with or for someone who you looked up to and admired a lot. Both of these people come under the category of managers and leaders. Not every great leader is a good manager, and not every great manager is a great leader. Isn't it confusing?

There is debate as to whether these two terms are the same or different. The majority of research has found that being a manager is more about your position, whereas being a leader is more about who you are.

You can be both a manager and a leader, or just one of them. Managership has nothing to do with leadership in general. Even if they are not in a powerful position inside a corporation or organization, a person might be a leader due to personal qualities.

A leader is one who influences the behaviour and work of others in group efforts, towards achievement of specified goals in a given situation. On the other hand, a manager can be effective *only* if he has got traits of a leader in them.

Managers at all levels are expected to lead work groups such that subordinates would happily follow their orders and accept their direction. A guy can be a leader because of all of his qualities. Being a manager is one of the various responsibilities that leaders have. Leaders are often seen in positions of authority, because they have the ability to persuade others to follow them. Anyone who has the ability to inspire and influence others can be a leader. Even if you are in an entry-level role, you can still exhibit leadership in the workplace. The key is to motivate others to do their best. Natural leaders tend to have strong speaking and listening skills and often attract the attention and respect of others irrespective of their roles or positions.

Jeff Bezos, founder and CEO of Amazon possesses a unique leadership skill in which he is capable of changing styles depending upon the people he is working with in the organization. Bezos's strong sense of humour and excellent strategic thinking has helped him make decisions on what he wants his employees to do and persuade them to do it well.

Bezos has also had a strong sense of self-awareness since his humble beginnings. He never openly set unrealistic goals. People told Bezos he was wasting his time and money when Amazon's trading activities were proving to be unprofitable. However, Bezos remained committed, confident and envisioned the massive success of Amazon in the long-term by seeking to offer a wide variety of products and services with low prices as well as fast and trusted delivery.

As a result, and as you can already see, Amazon has quickly risen to become the most trusted and powerful brand for consumers, sellers and creators. Bezos has always had a very influential leadership and effective managerial skills. He has always possessed a clear shared vision and objectives for Amazon by changing the way people perceive online shopping, expanding his company into the realm of entertainment as well (Amazon Prime, Amazon Music, etc.) This success showcases Bezos' strong interpersonal skills—such as motivating Amazon employees to develop and expand his business. It also represents Bezos' brilliant decision-making such that he was able to create a business empire from scratch and innovate his services as per rapidly evolving customer needs.

As a result, while leadership and management may appear to be distinct, they share many characteristics and are intertwined (as demonstrated by Bezos). If a manager is a good leader, his or her employees will be willing to follow his or her lead, trust him or her, and have a better working experience. Small business owners and entrepreneurs (like Jeff Bezos in his early days) frequently have to walk the line between being a leader and a manager, and management should strive to provide excellent leadership to those who work under them. Managers and leaders who combine the traits of each of these roles have a greater influence.

Here Are Some Traits Shared by Both Leaders and Managers

- Open communication
- Both have the primary focus of improving the organization
- Honesty
- They can both unlock the true potential of junior employees
- Delegation
- Integrity
- Decisiveness
- Respect
- Both act as role models to any institution or company
- Empathy
- Creativity
- Confidence
- Optimism
- Commitment
- Both may get involved in operational activities of the organization

1) **Communication:** Both leadership and management communication are crucial for an organization's success. Employees expect to be informed and educated on where their firm stands and where it is headed, as previously said. While leadership communication should motivate people, consistent and clear management communication encourages employees to accomplish their best work and strengthen team relationships.
2) **Interpersonal Skills:** Leaders have the ability to inspire and motivate others through positive interactions. Managers may be more focused on conflict resolution and team building. It's their job to ensure their team is getting along and can effectively collaborate. Both managers and leaders deal with

a plethora of varying personalities to achieve common goals, through collaboration and teamwork.
3) **Two-Way Learning:** The notion in two-way learning is that knowledge and advice can come from anywhere. This is necessary for managers and leaders to embrace ideas and insights from lower-level employees. It is critical to be eager and excited to listen to employees in order to be a great manager and leader. It's critical to realize that you can learn from anyone in the company, regardless of their position.
4) **Problem-Solving and Decision-Making:** Effective decision-making and problem-solving is both the manager's and the leader's responsibility. While leaders may be responsible for decision-making on a company-level, managers are held accountable for decision-making at the team or departmental level.
5) **Attention to Detail:** While managers use their attention to detail to point out flaws or issues, leaders use this skill to come up with innovative ideas or solutions. Being able to analyse different situations is an important skill for both managers and leaders to have.
6) **Change and Crisis Management:** Similar to decision making, leaders and managers should work collaboratively during times of change or crisis. The current world, after the Covid-19 Pandemic, has taught us about the importance of agile workplace transformation and the need to quickly adapt to change. While leaders may have a better understanding of the change that needs to be implemented, managers have better knowledge around how to enable their employees to accept the change and align with it.
7) **Team Players:** Managers and leaders know how to handle the team and direct the members to the right path to achieve the target. They know the strengths and weaknesses of team

members. Moreover, they use evaluation to keep things in order. Most importantly, they know how to handle conflicts.
8) **Conviction:** Both leadership and management require courage and confidence. They should be confident to know that they are taking the right steps to reach the goal. They are smart, quick-witted, flexible and take prompt action—rather than being cowardly or indecisive. After all, risks and innovative ideas often lead to higher rewards.
9) **Competence:** We all admire people who show high competence—whether they are precise craftsmen, world-class athletes or successful business leaders. They are present every day: the responsible people are always there when they are needed, but the highly competent ones take one step further. They are not just physically present, but they are ready to play no matter how they feel, what circumstances they face or how difficult the game is for them.

Effective managers and leaders inspire and motivate their teams to do the *same*, influencing workforce and organizational culture by setting an example. Great leaders and managers combine hard skills with high competence to take their organization to new levels of excellence and influence.
10) **Being the Backbone of a Company:** Both leadership and management are the establishment of a strong foundation and organized business structure. They both have the same end goal: to maximize profits and minimize costs—all the while ensuring maximum productivity and growth of their workforce. Thus, both leadership and management are essential elements of organizational achievements, where they work to actively identify what needs to be done, align resources with people and facilitate the achievement of goals.

Takeaways

- Exceptional leaders know how to multitask, and amongst these various tasks lie good old management.
- Contrary to popular belief, management and leadership are not identical.
- The management ensures the achievement of goals by following protocol, whereas the leader is a visionary who sets long-term goals.
- The manager ensures order and organization whereas the leader innovates and disrupts.
- However, leadership and management come together when it comes to communicating, handling diverse teams, achieving success and being the pillars of a firm.

6
MANAGE YOUR MANAGEMENT BETTER

We must find ways of convincing society as a whole, and those who train managers in particular, that the real leadership problems of our institutions—the getting things done, the implementation, the evolving of a consensus, the making of the right decisions at the right time with the right people is where the action is. Although we as a society haven't learned to give much credit to managers, I hope we can move toward recognizing that managerial and leadership jobs are among the most critical tasks of our society. As such, they deserve the professional status that we give to more traditional fields of knowledge.

—Professor Leonard R. Sayles

The previous chapter explored the complex relation between leadership and management. In this chapter, I'll explain the fundamentals of effective management (because, as we already know, great leaders are usually great managers too).

Management, in some form or another, is an integral part of living and is essential wherever human efforts are to be undertaken to achieve desired objectives. Whether we're managing our lives or our businesses, the basic principles of management are always in play. Consider the managerial function of a simple housewife and how she employs the managerial ingredients in her household management. She begins by assessing her household and its requirements. She anticipates the household's requirements for a week, a month or longer. She assesses her resources as well as any limitations she may face. She organizes and plans her resources so that she may get the most out of them. She keeps track of the family's budget, expenses and other activities. In a large home, she shares the work and coordinates the activity of the other members. She inspires and encourages them to complete their tasks to the best of their abilities. She is always looking for ways to develop herself, and she discusses her objectives, resources and methods for achieving them. Even in the workplace, these ingredients are the essential functions of management. Isn't it simple?

Many management philosophers have their own definitions of management. For example, Van Fleet and Peterson define management as, 'A set of activities directed at the efficient and effective utilization of resources in the pursuit of one or more goals.'

Basically, management is the act of getting people together to accomplish desired goals and objectives using available resources efficiently and effectively. Management can also be described as human effort, including design, to support the development of meaningful outputs from a system, since organizations can be considered as systems.

Good managers are always looking for ways to streamline their businesses so that they can make a profit. To put it another way, good managers are required to keep their businesses on track by ensuring that everything they do is ethically aimed toward offering what customers desire. A good manager is responsible for reducing waste and uncertainty, controlling costs and motivating employees to do the same. Similarly, excellent managers take calculated risks and exercise sound judgement on a frequent basis (which becomes the basis of entrepreneurship).

Because most managers are in charge of more work than a single person can ordinarily handle, a smart manager delegates and integrates his or her responsibilities (or the work of others). A manager accomplishes this by serving as a clear line of communication inside the company. As a result, good management is required to infuse drive, innovation, discipline and excitement into areas where they are either absent or insignificant.

Perhaps, the importance of management was highlighted by the late President of the United States, John F. Kennedy when he said that, 'The role of management in our society is critical in human progress. It serves to identify a great need of our time: to improve standards of living for all people through the effective utilization of human and material sources.'

Good management becomes the backbone of successful organizations and brilliant leadership. Managing life means getting things done to achieve life's objectives, and managing an organization means getting things done with and through other people to achieve its objectives. Management is an art of knowing what to do when to do and see that it is done in the best and cheapest way.

How about you save yourself from a heavy introductory MBA class and instead, go through these points below to understand the basics of management?

- **Management is *both*: an art and a science.** Management is science because of several reasons. It is universally accepted, it follows a cause-and-effect relationship, etc.; and at the same time, it is an art, because management requires perfection through experience, practical knowledge, creativity, personal skills and emotional intelligence.

- **Management basically equates to organizing work.** In a very basic sense, management is nothing but the process of organizing activities of people working towards some common purpose.

    For example, if the objective of a company is to sell 10,000 mobile phones, then the manager will take the action, motivate all the employees and organize all the resources keeping in mind the main target of selling 10,000 mobile phones.

- **Management is multi-layered.** It involves the management of work, people and operations. The majority of management is in charge of a company or organization's service or production cycle. Managers collaborate closely with and advise members of their teams. A manager views each employee as a person with unique requirements—as well as a member of a bigger team. Managers must persuade their team members to use their own strengths to achieve the organization's objectives in order to be effective.

- **Management is all-pervasive.** Management is a phenomenon that occurs all around the world. Management can be used in profit-making, non-profit-making, commercial or non-business organizations; even a hospital, school, club or housing must be managed efficiently. Management is employed all throughout the world, whether in the United States, the United Kingdom or India.

- **Management is a goal-oriented process.** An essential aspect of management is to combine individual efforts and direct them towards achieving organizational goals. These objectives differ from one organization to the next. For example, a

commercial motivation can exist in an organization, yet a social work organization's goal may be to eliminate illiteracy among children. Management is aware of these objectives and is working to achieve them.
- **Management involves team work.** Management is the combination of teamwork and leadership, where all the team members work together to run an organization in effective ways and all members take complete ownership. Good management can achieve what an individual cannot achieve. Think about it: an organization wants to launch a new product. In this product, the designing team will create the product, the marketing team will advertise, sales team helps in advertising and selling the product, and only then will the product be finally launched and will garner profits.
- **Management is never-ending.** From planning, organizing, staffing, directing and controlling a company's operations, all management functions are conducted continually. Managers undertake a variety of duties in the organization on a constant basis, depending on what is expected of them.
- ***And* it is ever-changing.** In order to succeed, a company must adapt to its surroundings. As a result, management is dynamic in nature, adapting to changing social, economic, and political circumstances. McDonald's, for example, had to adapt its menu in order to service and emerge as a major fast-food powerhouse in the Indian market.

    Management establishes plans, policies and decisions based on the circumstances. Possibilities for management based on circumstances. Another example would be—during Christmas, organizations give a high discount to customers to maximize sales. So, a manager is supposed make plans to sell their products more accordingly to the prevailing situation.
- **It is an intangible energy.** Although the management

function cannot be seen, its presence can be felt. The orderliness and coordination in the workplace can be felt as a sign of the management's presence. Mismanagement is simpler to detect since it causes chaos and confusion within the organization.
- **Management needs *a lot of* leadership.** Management includes leadership because a manager has to lead a group of people, community or organization to get desired outcomes. A manager must be capable of motivating and inspiring the confidence of the workforce and hence, be a charismatic leader.

How Can You Be an Effective Manager?

1) **Understand your role as a manager.** You need to achieve the business goals set for you and provide an environment that allows your team to be effective and satisfied while developing their potential.
2) ***And* of course, understand the roles of *others*.** This requires a clear understanding of their accountabilities, authorities and the nature of these working relationships.
3) **Know your peers/team well.** Get to know your employees personally and what they want in life. Take the time to get to know them both on a personal level and a professional level. Know their career goals, but also know their personal interests and passions.
4) **Weave these peers into a solid team.** Effective teamwork requires a shared understanding of the purpose of the team and the shared goals. The duty of a manager is to encourage a good flow of information in all directions.
5) **Deal with this solid team empathetically.** Empathetic managers are aware of their employees' feelings. They have

a good understanding of how their teammates are feeling, which allows them to communicate effectively and solve difficulties quickly. As a result, their employees have greater faith in them, and managers have more opportunities to create rapport, which fuels team performance. Good managers who are empathic with their staff are better able to create personal links and foster long-term partnerships with them.

6) **Set realistic goals.** Every employee must have something to work for, and therefore, it is the duty of a manager to set goals that his subordinate will strive for. Not only will these goals give the employees a new purpose and direction, they will also ensure that all employees are marching towards the larger organizational goals.

7) **Talk it out.** Try to be forthcoming with your team. Let them know pertinent information and realize the effects that lack of communication can have on your staff. A skilled project manager ensures that nothing slips between the cracks, from handling team meetings with poise to providing individuals with the proper direction in the project. They are not hesitant to use existing resources such as online communication platforms to do this.

8) **Be approachable.** It's quite acceptable to be friends with your employees. Just because you're a manager doesn't mean you have to be cold and hostile. Doing so would make you unapproachable and disliked by your staff, which is something you definitely don't want. While it's critical that your employees understand you're in charge, engage with them, have fun with them and make your company a fantastic place to work.

When an employee needs to talk to you, you must make sure that you make time to see him and step aside for a discussion. It is okay to put your work on the back-burner for a moment and focus on this person in need of your assistance.

9) **Delegate tasks carefully.** Delegating work—assigning responsibilities and tasks to your employees—is the cornerstone to effective management. Most bosses believe they must supervise every action taken by their staff, which can be terrible in your position. You multiply the amount of work that can be performed by delegating work to your staff. You're also assisting in the development of your employees' competencies, leadership skills and self-confidence.

10) **Bring out the best of your employees (through appraisal and constructive criticism).** The finest managers are always aware of good performance and offer recognition where credit is due. Even when they find flaws or shortcomings, they criticize constructively in order for employees to see their errors and work hard to remedy them.

Thanking your staff for their contributions and recognizing them for a job well done can boost their morale significantly. Even the tiniest accomplishments must be celebrated at first. Believe in your team even if no one else does, and you will certainly bring out the best in them. Isn't that, after all, what true leadership is all about?

Just like you, every other person is hungry for appreciation, especially at the workplace. All employees are, at some point or the other, seeking praise for the work they do. That way, they feel valued, more confident and hence, more driven to achieve goals.

11) **Keep your word.** This sounds simple enough but—sometimes—is more difficult than you may think on the surface. Sometimes, we have the best intentions to do what we say, but other things arise which are outside our

control that can prevent us from fulfilling our pledges and commitments.

Be careful when making promises. If you, as a leader, do not have complete control over an outcome, don't make the promise. It is perfectly alright to say to your teams and employees, 'I will do my best', but when you make a promise, your employees will expect you to keep it. Excuses, even if totally legit, only breeds distrust.

12) **Be tech-savvy.** Smart managers know that technology (like project management software or online collaboration tools), is there to simplify the way they handle their teams and the way their teams manage their work. They understand that technology has a solution for everything, from effective work management and collaboration to simple reporting and time monitoring. This is why they never hesitate to invest in cutting-edge technology. In fact, they are the first to seek out technological solutions that would make life easier for their workers and increase productivity. They are valued by everyone, since they are able to reduce distractions while simultaneously bringing the most out of each team member.

Things You *Do Not* Want to Do to Be an Effective Manager

- **Don't take criticism personally.** It is human nature for each of us not to like criticism—especially when it is said *behind* our backs. However, I encourage you not to overreact. If you are in a leadership position, you are going to be talked about. It sometimes gets lonely at the top, you must accept that. The 'water cooler' or 'cafeteria talk' will be positive, and sometimes it will not be positive in the least. You may not like what you hear, and it can affect your own performance and leadership. If you are not intended to hear the conversation, don't try to include yourself in that conversation.

Remember, you are not going to always please everyone as a manager and leader. Sometimes, you will have to make decisions that will not be easy to swallow. We should always consult our teams when we make decisions that affect the team, but sometimes as managers and leaders, we too have little choice in decisions that are made. Keep that in mind, and don't hold your employees to a higher standard than you are holding yourself to.

- **Don't dismiss your employees' ideas.** Brainstorming solutions to a particular problem or situation or encouraging your team to come up with ideas as to how working practises may be improved creates a sense of inclusion and can often encourage useful suggestions that might not otherwise have been considered. Once again, try seeing your team members as equal partakers and equally intelligent when it comes to suggestions.

- **Don't try to act perfect.** Letting your employees know that you messed up or that you were wrong about something doesn't make you a bad manager. In fact, your imperfections and humility will make you a more likeable and relatable manager/team leader.

  Furthermore, being a manager does not imply that you must be an expert on everything. It's fine to just say, 'I don't know,' and to be open to having your team members enlighten and tell you about things from time to time. Your employees, believe me, want to know that their bosses are human, that they make errors and fail occasionally.

- **Don't take credit for your employees' work, *please*.** Taking credit for someone else's work is one of the worst things you can do as an employee or a manager. I refer to it as

'Intellectual Theft'. This type of activity will absolutely destroy teamwork and foster resentment and foment an environment of distrust. Before you become tempted in taking credit for someone else's work, ask yourself how you would feel if the roles were reversed. Would you be angry? Would you feel unappreciated, dejected and despondent? If so, why would you want to do this to someone else?

- **Don't lie.** Even if it's for a good purpose, don't distort the truth, suppress information or make things up. Strive for openness: if you keep your employees in the dark, they will lose faith in you. Say something if it's not working out. Let folks know when things are going well. Share your concerns when you have them. If you need something done by next week and are scared it won't get done, talk to your team about it. Have uncomfortable conversations with people and tell them what's on your mind. Just don't try to control people's behaviour or feelings by manipulating them.
- **Don't micromanage.** Don't delegate minor tasks and then micromanage the person by constantly looking over his or her shoulder, and don't be in a rush to take away responsibilities as soon as there's a problem. Nobody likes being pestered all the time and treated like a baby.

  Instead, empower people to succeed. Delegate broader responsibilities while providing clear direction and training on the 'how', 'what' and 'why'. Help your team develop personal accountability.
- **Don't be *too* detached.** This one's the stark opposite of micromanagement—but *equally* damaging. Detached managers don't provide much direction and often leave employees to their own devices on projects. Some don't even try to understand the day-to-day processes of their employees; therefore, they don't provide insight or help. This can be

frustrating for employees who feel as though they are on an island with no guidance or nobody to call out to for help.
- **Don't lash out.** I previously worked for a CEO that would make the mistake of holding his scheduled meetings even if he was in the throes of anger. He would stand up and start off by attempting to appear calm and rational, but it did not take long before his face would turn red and he would start ranting and raving about anything and everything.

  If anyone dared to ask him a question while he was in this condition, he would turn even more red and start hurling condescending insults. After these meetings, it would take me *hours* to try and calm everyone's nerves and prevent them from walking out. I am sorry to say that I was not always successful.

  Take a time out for yourself and calm yourself down before talking to others. Better to postpone a meeting or excuse yourself before you make yourself and everyone else uncomfortable. This goes for one-on-one conversations as well as group meetings.

  If others do not see you in control of your emotions, it will not take long for the condition to spread and infect your team(s).
- **Don't be biased.** Providing rewards to individuals and recognition for jobs well done is one manner of positive re-enforcement and public acknowledgement. However, too much individual achievement recognition can actually decrease morale rather than enhancing it. Most of us have seen too many instances where this has created situations where team members (because of their position and lack of visibility) created 'me first!' type individualistic attitudes and breeding of internal resentment.

  You already know, *no* leader or manager can be successful

without a successful team. In fact, it can be well said that a leader or manager is only as strong as the team he works with and develops. I would strongly suggest that when you or your direct subordinates are up for any reward, you instil in them the need to share that wealth with the individual team members and contributors.

- **Don't make undue/unrealistic demands.** Simple: it makes you come across as someone selfish and lacking empathy. Don't make your employees execute a physically difficult activity just because your irrational boss insisted on it. Negotiate with your boss and commit to appropriate outcomes to find ways to manage the demand. Then provide your team the resources and support they need to reach, if not surpass, their goals.
- **Don't blurt out threats.** Threatening and intimidating others in any way is a mark of a weak leader. By creating a good work atmosphere that enables individuals to engage with enthusiasm and purpose, a great leader can build team and individual commitment. Without using threats, you can address employee responsibilities and repercussions, both positive and negative.
- **Don't do stuff all by yourself, of course.** You are a manager for a reason. You are there to help manage the team towards victory. Of course, especially in a start-up, you might be required to do intermediary tasks. While this might be the case, make sure that you don't try to do it all by yourself. Instead, mediate tasks to your team and delegate work.
- **Don't criticize a team member in front of the entire team.** Why? It's humiliating! If you have a problem with a team member's attitude or performance, don't bring it up in front of the entire team. Instead, take them aside for a private one-on-one conversation away from the office. Else, they

might believe you have personal prejudices and are targeting them for no reason; that'll cause resentment and naturally, lesser productivity.
- **Don't shirk accountability:** Ultimately, as a leader or manager, the responsibility for your team and their actions, mistakes, successes and failures rests with you. Finger-pointing, undue criticism and passing the buck in order to protect your own interests ahead of those of the wider team will ultimately destroy morale and may call into question your integrity and ability as a team leader. Cowards run away from taking responsibility after failures; brave, confident leaders embrace those failures and learn from them.

Takeaways

- Management is a major role taken up by most budding and established leaders.
- Management is necessary to achieve goals.
- Management involves dealing with various situations and people.
- Good managers are great communicators, honest, approachable, empathetic and well-versed with technology.
- Bad managers, however, shirk responsibility, do not communicate, play the blame-game, lack soft skills and break team spirit. Don't be a bad manager if you want to be a great leader.

7

SPEAK UP (LIKE A BOSS)

Oratory is the masterful art. Poetry, painting, music, sculpture, architecture please, thrill, inspire - but oratory rules. The orator dominates those who hear him, convinces their reason, controls their judgment, compels their action. For the time being, he is master.

—David Josiah Brewer, Former Associate Justice of the Supreme Court of the United States

Winston Churchill, Abraham Lincoln, Mahatma Gandhi, Franklin D. Roosevelt, John F. Kennedy, Ronald Reagan and Martin Luther King Junior; the world's most captivating leaders share a few things in common—great ideas, courage and of course, brilliant oration. They were willing to speak out at a time when others weren't. They also communicated a feeling so powerful that their words have been impossible to forget. A competent orator has a dominating appearance, knows how to make an entrance and appears aspirational. A good orator has good body language as well. He won't slouch, stammer or speak with his hands in his pockets. These minor things may appear insignificant, yet they are crucial. And yes, a good orator makes a great leader. We all already know this about the most powerful, unforgettable leaders across history and cultures. In today's time, we get thrilled at the powerful voice of Steve Jobs, listen with delight to the eloquence of Barack Obama or cringe heavily at the speeches and remarks of Donald Trump.

Many aspects of leadership have to do with performance—and high on the list is the need to speak powerfully. This could include aspects of a leader's 'voice', such as articulating a vision and showing sympathy for his or her followers. In terms of vocal force, subtlety and variety of expression, it's also literal.

You may occupy the position, but you lack power. People may be required to follow your directions if you sit behind the boss's desk, but they are not required to show up with excitement or demonstrate long-term devotion. Leaders, on the other hand, have more power when it comes to making decisions.

Effective communication is no longer described as a two-way street. Leaders need to know a lot more than the mechanics of sending and receiving information, because communication is much more complicated for them. Harnessing the ability to communicate effectively is one of the most important skills a leader can have.

You've heard this axiom from motivational speakers and read it in books: 'You don't need a title to be a leader.'

But what you do need are the communication skills to influence someone to follow you—to accept your ideas, to sign off on the proposed action, to fund the project and to encourage their network to 'show up' for you.

Effective leadership requires verbal discipline. Leaders need to care about and practise the quality, specificity and power of their language. Not enough of them do. It's critical. A competent leader's ability to communicate effectively is a vital leadership function and a key attribute. Effective communication and leadership are inextricably linked. In order to produce achievements through others, you must be a great communicator in many relationships at the organizational level, in communities and groups and occasionally on a worldwide scale.

Sounding like a leader means you're communicating in a way that inspires people to aspire to bigger things. To give it their all and to be the best they can be. Embrace your ideas and follow your intuition—whether or not you have a formal title. You don't have to be a great orator or produce charismatic talks. It's more about how you come across in all of your communications, including what you say (and write) on a daily basis. Best of all, you have complete control over how you speak, write and communicate. You don't need to be in a senior position or have the right task. Every day, from where you sit right now, you can make a difference.

You must think clearly, articulate ideas and exchange knowledge with a wide range of people. You must learn to handle the rapid flows of information within the organization and among customers, partners, employees, and other stakeholders and influencers.

A leader's language is different! Language used in a leadership role serves a distinct function than language used in a non-leadership role. Your communication is responsible for instilling purpose and inspiration, as well as providing meaning about the present and future, explaining complex trade-offs, demonstrating resolve in the face of adversity, articulating matters that others do not see, and calling on the organization to uphold commitments and standards. This does not happen when the language is bland, casual or ambiguous. True leadership elicits change while maintaining a safety net of stability, gives support while also challenging, knows when to confront and when to lie low, and decides when to directly state or indirectly imply.

How Then, Do You Sound Like a Real Leader?

1) **Monitor how you speak, first and foremost.** What words and phrases would be on your 'soundtrack' if you had a recording of yourself in the last 24 hours? Are you more likely to criticize and complain, or are you more likely to encourage others (and yourself) to experiment and innovate? How often do you tell others what they should do instead of assisting them in their development and growth? To what extent do your words open up rather than close down the spectrum of possibilities?

    If your language is littered with the words 'no', 'but', 'can't' and a slew of other complaints, it's time to take a closer look at how your music is being received by others. This is an extremely important aspect of your personal brand and reputation—and it has everything to do with how you sound as a leader.

2) **Put yourself out there.** If you want to communicate well, don't be out of sight. Don't limit yourself to your emails and official correspondence. Be available, visible and present. Putting yourself out there—consistently and predictably—shows others who you are as a leader. To feel linked to the task you want people to accomplish, they need to see and feel who you are. Even (and especially) when speaking amid a crisis, find opportunities to communicate with all of your stakeholder groups. This helps create your strong personal leadership branding.

3) **Engage with your audience.** Nerves and self-consciousness are common side effects of keynote speaking—or speaking in any high-stakes setting. It almost probably causes an adrenaline rush in the system. This might cause a speaker to rush through a speech, giving strict attention to the content

to be delivered but missing the audience connection.

It was the moderator of the panel discussions (rather than the keynote speakers) who took the time to create a connection with her listeners at one conference I attended early in my career. She told a story about her mother, another about herself in grade school and a third about a close relationship with someone who should have been her adversary. Even the brilliant speaker (the one who created buzz) didn't accomplish this key task. So, ask yourself: do you want to be recognized as an expert who maintains his or her distance or one who knows how to engage listeners with warmth and humour—even in the midst of all that expertise and tension?

4) **Control the fillers.** I know it's difficult, but during pauses in a speech or presentation, do not fill the silence with nonsensical sub-vocalizations like 'um', 'er', 'you know', 'like', 'frankly' or 'to be honest'. It merely adds to the awkwardness of the silence. A subconscious repetitive cough, lip-licking, or overused hand gesture are all examples of this. Fillers, both verbal and nonverbal, can be distracting and damage your credibility. Instead, pause, take a breath, clear your mind and begin afresh.

5) **Plan what you have to say.** Think about the terms you'll use before your next leadership event. Be specific, concrete and vivid in your writing. Rehearse in front of a trusted audience: how did it sound to them? By definition, leadership language must be heightened and bold. You must feel at ease with these conditions. Too many leaders are stumped for words because they have no idea what they desire. 'What's going on here, and what do I want?' ask yourself before speaking (formally or informally). You'll have a better chance of speaking to these wider needs and aspirations if your answer is based on

the organization's shared purpose rather than your personal desires. If you don't know what you want (or worse, want to pursue selfish goals), you should remain silent until you are prepared to articulate the wider view of your team or company.

6) *But* **don't forget to be raw and authentic.** What distinguishes a leader from a regular person? A leader is aware of who they are as a human being. Be truthful and sincere. Find your own voice and stop speaking in corporate jargon or sounding like someone you aren't. Allow your communication to reflect who you are, where you came from and what you value. Authentic leadership is something that others want, appreciate and will follow. So, instead of worrying about performative eloquence, focus on being genuine. Don't try to hide your true self. People will never gladly follow someone who appears to be insincere or fake.

7) **Showcase confidence (that's approachable and not cocky).** This one's important; listen carefully. Your words should show an air of confidence that lets others believe in you as a person and put stock in what you say. However, it also allows for others to feel as though they can bring up their own ideas and beliefs without thinking you will shut them down. In other words, they feel they can approach you as their leader. This is critical for effective leadership. Because a fundamental goal of every leader is to open new doors and inspire good change in people and the business as a whole.

Leaders are sometimes portrayed as commanding certain duties or dictating what should be done next. However, the exceptional leaders use the skill of coaching and guiding, to empower those they lead. Get to know the people who work under you as people first. They're not just your workers, they're human beings with different dreams, goals and skills. Find out what their skills are, and then invite them to participate in a debate about their own ideas and perspectives on a topic. This will provide the impression of a collaborative effort, rather than a hierarchical organization in which what you say is the final word. The most important purpose of speaking like a leader is to show others that you are concerned about their well-being.

8) **Avoid lazy language.** Leaders sometimes 'pull back' by qualifying their speech: 'It's sort of up to this team,' or 'This is kind of a tough situation.' Resist the temptation of this lazy language.

   Using clear language will increase your courage by more fully connecting you to what you need and want to say. Call an object by its proper name and a situation *as it is*. It is always prudent to stay warned about 'wishy-washy throwaway phrases' that we work into our speech to be polite or build consensus. Examples include 'perhaps', 'kind of', 'hopefully' or any other derivative of the same. Such limp words will only weaken you and your status as a leader. Deliberately use concrete and accurate language, and clarity will follow.

9) **Take it nice and slow.** As mentioned above, verbal pauses at the end of a sentence (not filled by useless words) can make us sound more powerful. People will lean in to listen to what comes next. Pausing makes you seem confident; using fillers make you seem nervous. If someone cuts you off during the break, smile warmly and say (in a non-confrontational way), 'Actually, I was not finished.' Then resume.

10) **Don't formulate your thoughts in a haste.** Simply take your time to demonstrate that you're a leader who's at ease in

front of the orating spotlight. Too many speakers do not. Even when he or she has been working hard while listeners have been sitting still and nibbling on popcorn—doodling or dreaming about a deep-dish pizza—the breathless presenter is the one who exhausts the audience. Whatever comes to mind.

The actor's world has a fantastic device for teaching us how to do this. Beats is the term for this concept. A character's intention is represented by a beat, which the actor performs until the intention is realized or frustrated, at which point another beat begins. You can use the same device in terms of your main points: where do you finish one, and begin the next one? These are the places where you should pay special attention to pausing and letting your audience take a mental breath. Pause. Allow the audience to breathe. See how it works? Listeners will both relax and follow you more easily.

11) **The magic of positive vocabulary.** I had developed the habit of complaining as a teenager, whether it was over too much schoolwork, an irritating teacher, or a physics lab partner who didn't perform their fair share of the job. Finally, my parents had had enough of listening to my whining. That's when my father offered me the advice that helped me sound like a leader and advance in my job several times. 'Son, try using only positive words,' he simply suggested.

When I took on that challenge, it changed everything. I found it impossible to complain when using only positive words and immediately became someone people wanted to be around because they felt positive. Instead of, 'Why did you do that?' it was 'Tell me what happened.' I replaced 'No, but…' with 'Yes, and…'; and 'We can't…' with 'What if…'

These small adjustments not only helped me seem more

like a leader, but they also made me feel more cheerful, powerful, creative, and open to new possibilities—and it was contagious to everyone around me. It resulted in a positive feedback loop.

12) **Don't use dragged out, loaded sentences.** Putting only one thought in a sentence helps eliminate most of the above-mentioned issues. Verbal pauses between sentences can become powerful attention grabbers when we isolate one concept per sentence. If each sentence has a single, concise notion, the danger of committing a verbal error is also reduced. Furthermore, a sharp thought pierces through unnecessary qualifiers and phrases.

13) **It is okay to use 'but',** *but* **use it carefully.** 'But' is a contradictory conjunction, and should not be used after a positive phrase if your intention is to be positive. Often, 'but' signals that whatever came before is not wholly valid. 'I liked your project, but...' is a popular phrase. The speaker casts doubt on the genuineness of what was 'liked' and emphasizes what he or she wishes to change. When a leader says, 'Thanks for the feedback, but I think...' it usually means, 'I don't value what you said, and we'll do it my way.' 'I've weighed your criticism and remain confident in my judgement,' is a better phrase to use. Similarly, a leader will address a team, 'This group did great work last quarter, but now we have to focus.' Better to say, 'Your great work last quarter is just the momentum we need, because this quarter will be a bigger challenge.' Instead of 'but', use 'and', 'however', 'yet', 'except' or 'that said'.

14) **Let loose.** The desire to be seen as knowledgeable and dynamic usually makes us tighten up, making us seem boring, grim and unapproachable. Staying loose physically and mentally instead can give exactly the opposite impression. Besides,

if you don't know something, you won't suddenly acquire that knowledge through a burning desire when you're in the spotlight. Observe speakers at *any* conference you attend. Do they give the impression of looseness, of ease and a light touch? Then think about your own performances. If you're in doubt, enlist the aid of those performance friends—the mirror and video camera—who, as always, are happy to lend their advice and support.

15) **Because you are only human, after all.** You have a lot of experience guiding what you're managing as a leader. This does not, however, imply that you have met every possible unique circumstance. As a result, another important advice for communicating like a leader is to avoid making the assumption that you know everything. As a leader, it is OK to ask another individual a question; this demonstrates that you are human and promotes your approachability. Practise short 30-second to 1-minute presentations at home about previous experiences you've had. Talk out loud so you can give a succinct but authentic example of what you've done in the past and how it will affect the current situation or project.

16) **Don't go overboard with the superlatives.** When a lot of things are called 'amazing', 'awesome', 'unbelievable', 'epic' or 'fantastic', very little of them are. Superlatives that are overused destroy actual meaning.

When a leader declares ordinary events to be extraordinary on a regular basis, he or she adds to a pattern of everything sounding the same. Rather than making broad statements, explain the action and reaction in basic terms. Instead of calling the sales presentation 'amazing', talk about it being 'clear', 'compelling', 'well-researched', 'full of the right data' and so on. Also, refrain from using a generic 'awesome' to describe the team (did they inspire awe?) Instead, say, 'Excellent work.'

17) **'We' rather than 'I'.** Do not make it about yourself, even while using language that talks about your experiences. Instead, it is most likely the past experiences involved other people, so use 'we' statements. 'We' statements make everyone feel included and also take the spotlight off yourself. Instead of, 'After this issue came up, I went through our data and developed a different model to X,' replace 'I' with 'we'. Even if you drove that idea in the past, that is not the point of you sharing this experience. The point is to foster a team effort in creating an idea or plan for a current situation in which you sharing this past experience might improve that plan.

18) **Break monotony by playing with your voice.** Make sure you vary with your pitch. If you have a loud personality, lower your voice to drive home a message. That way, you surprise your audience and capture their attention instantly. If you are quiet, enunciate and speak up. Also, do not use a monotone voice (it will bore people), but make sure you are not going in pitch overdrive either (you do not want to sound like Dory).

19) **Speak proudly.** Stand up straight; it opens your vocal tract so that you can speak from your diaphragm. This way, you create a stronger voice as well as a commanding presence. You do not want people to lean in to hear what you say because they cannot understand you. You want people to lean in to hear what you say because they are intrigued. Do not be obnoxiously loud either; aim for the right volume (and confidence).

20) **Have conviction in your ideas.** Because if *you* won't, how will others?

Yes, I know you already are convinced by your own ideas—but do you show it? Consider the figures we know as passionate speakers: Martin Luther King, Jr. of 'I Have a Dream', Ronald Reagan of 'Tear down this wall!' and Dr Jill Bolte Taylor of 'My Stroke of Insight' in her TED Talk. These speakers weren't just delivering words; they were living them as they spoke. A major distinction between stage performers and public speakers has little to do with knowledge, passion or even devotion. It does, however, have a lot to do with how those things are presented. If you're not a passionate speaker (and by now you should know this about yourself), work on how you can externalize your emotional responses. That's what performers and leaders are trained to do. And that's what your audience is depending upon you to do as well, so they can be as turned on by your ideas as you are.

21) **Charm them with your empathy.** In speaking like a leader, you will want to convey support, but also have the goal of helping those you lead reach their potential. One skill to conveying support is providing affective responses.

A person may be sending off vibes of certain emotions, and as the leader, it is important for you to pick up on those emotions and respond in a manner that provides support but also maintains the productivity you need in leading a team. An appropriate affective response validates the expression of an emotion, because neglecting emotion makes someone feel uncared for, which might damage the trust you built in the first place. Simply acknowledging the person's emotion is one method. 'Terry, I saw you seemed a little low today, let me know if you need anything,' for example. This remark confirms that you are aware of and concerned about this person's emotional display, but it does not delve into any particular specifics. It does, however, provide you with a window of opportunity to offer assistance.

22) **Don't let verbal errors stop you.** If you make a mistake in a sentence or fumble over words during a presentation or speech, don't stop and apologize. Do not cringe, stiffen up or click your tongue at the same time.

    Carry on as if nothing has happened. Most people aren't aware of these kinds of verbal errors (unless you make them). Stopping and apologizing will draw unnecessary attention to it. You both confuse the audience and yourself. Just make sure the message is clear in general.

23) **Stand tall.** Stand with your feet flat on the floor, at the width of your armpits or shoulders. You'll appear steady, steadfast and strong. If you're using a lectern, your notes will be sitting on the top, so your hands will be free. Use them. And if you feel the urge to move away from that piece of furniture, by all means, do that too. A speaker who steps away from the lectern from time to time appears completely at ease—an essential attribute in a leader addressing an audience/team.

Here's a Small Pool of Words and Phrases Exceptional Leaders Say Often

- 'Let's do this!' At some point, it's not enough to stand on the side-lines and ask questions. When deadlines are approaching or time is of the essence, strong leaders speak up to motivate their teams to take action before it's too late. It's helpful to remind them that you're willing to roll up your sleeves and provide a hand if they're anxious or stretched.
- '**I have good news *and* bad news.**' You might wonder

why this would be motivating. Have you ever worked for a management team that kept everything behind closed doors? Leaders who swept their responsibilities under the rug? Leaders who are effective do the exact opposite. They are truth tellers who explain who, what, where, when and why they made their decisions. The ability of a leader to communicate both good and bad news honestly and openly goes a long way toward motivating people and earning their trust.

- **'What are your thoughts (on this)?'** Many leaders are far too quick in directing and/or sharing their thoughts on how to proceed forward with their employees. Leaders don't produce followers; they generate more leaders. I think that one of every leader's key goals should be to develop other leaders. You won't be able to do this until you give your employees the freedom to use their judgement to solve their own problems. When I communicate with my team, I make it a point to listen to them out before expressing my opinion on a topic.
- **'I'm listening…tell me more.'** Saying this sentence relaxes people since it demonstrates that you care about what they're seeing, thinking and experiencing. Frequently, supervisors deliver the message that their employees must be as productive as possible at all times. Allowing people to share more than the pressing daily issues, on the other hand, encourages them to delve deeper. 'Taking the time to utilize those three words with people once a week altered everything about our business,' one superior I worked with once said. 'I learnt the majority of what I know after I posed the question, not before.'
- **'Can you show me?'** While asking for help is admirable, the ideal method to ask help is to request to be shown.

Why? Advice is only useful for a short time. Knowledge lasts a lifetime. Knowing how to perform anything is quite important. Don't just ask for suggestions. Inquire about being shown. Request that you be trained. Inquire about being shown. Over time, you'll see that your employees do the same thing, which will contribute to a culture where everyone learns, grows and develops. This will also assist you in developing and nurturing future leaders. That's a win in my book.

- **'I will need everyone's help (in achieving this).'** Sure, you're the boss. You're in charge. And maybe you really do have all the answers (although that's incredibly unlikely). But even superheroes need help, don't they?

    Asking for help shows vulnerability, respect and a willingness to listen—all qualities of a great leader. And all are qualities you hope your staff exhibits. Trust me, you won't lose respect. You'll gain respect. And you'll implicitly compliment the skills, knowledge and experience of the person you ask.

- **'Yes.'** Your team is busy. Their plates are already full. There are plenty of reasons to sit tight, stay secure and preserve things as they are when your staff have new ideas. Say yes to something different every day. Accept a challenge and take a chance. Accept the employee who is enthusiastic about a fresh concept. And absolutely say yes to the employee who is hesitant to bring up their fresh idea, because hearing 'yes' will enhance their confidence and self-esteem. Remember that when you say 'yes', what you're really saying is, 'I trust you.' Isn't that exactly what every employee hopes to hear?

- ***And* 'No'.** (I might sound like I'm contradicting myself, however, stay tuned for my explanation.) Even though 'yes' is incredibly powerful, you can't do everything. You can't help everyone. You may want to—but you can't. Sometimes, you just need to say no. So, say it. Don't say 'maybe'—unless you mean it. Don't say, 'We'll look at that down the road,' unless you mean it. If it really is no, say 'no'. As a leader, your job is to make decisions. So, make decisions, and always explain why you made that decision. While other people might not agree with your reasoning, at least they'll understand that you do have reasons.

- **'Could I provide some feedback?'** Great leaders do not shy away from giving feedback, and they offer it in a compassionate way. Starting the conversation by asking permission to give feedback allows the employee to psychologically engage and hear the feedback from a better place.

> - What are your observations about the situation and how you showed up?
> - What options might exist to move forward and respond differently in the future?
> - What part of that feedback felt true for you?
> - What actions do you want to take given this conversation?

- **'How can I help?'** Effective leaders are servant leaders. They meet the needs of those in their tribe by removing obstacles from their way and ensuring that they are set up for success. They also hold them accountable for achieving the same level of achievement, which is a rather high standard. But it all begins with the human trait of concern and care. And the first question they usually ask is, 'What do you need from me so you can succeed?'
- **'We might be going wrong somewhere.'** Albert Einstein once said, 'Problems cannot be solved with the same mindset that created them.' To put it another way, learn to question

your own thinking, and urge your employees to do the same. It will assist people in taking a more holistic approach to situations and examining them from all angles, resulting in more creative outcomes.

- **'This was my mistake.'** Effective leaders aren't hiding behind their own hubris or status and deflecting responsibility to someone else. They are accountable to others and own up to making mistakes, which sets the example for their tribe to be honest and not fear making their own mistakes. This also encourages your employees owning up to their mistakes, without you having to point it out or without any blame-games in your team.
- **'Great!'** No one gets tired of praise. Pick someone—pick as many people as possible—who did something well and say, 'That was great how you....' Praise is one of the best—and easiest—gifts you can give. Praise costs you nothing, yet it can be priceless to the one receiving it. And it feels really good to give, because you usually get one right back. A win-win.
- **'I trust your abilities.'** Effective leaders can say this with certainty because they believe in and trust their employees' skills to complete the task. They'll get out of the way and let people own their work, allowing them to use their God-given brains to create and innovate. This is why Steve Jobs once said, 'It doesn't make sense to hire smart people and tell them what to do; we hire smart people so they can tell us what to do.'
- **'We will solve this together.'** When big problems happen, great managers reassure their people without resorting to fake optimism. They don't make promises they can't keep. This phrase reminds everyone that they have built-in resilience and can struggle through the hard times without giving up or giving in. Plus, saying 'we' adds a sense of camaraderie.

- **'We are a team!'** As team leader, it may seem obvious to you, and perhaps even to the people on your team, that you are a unit that needs to work together to be most effective. However, I feel it goes a long way to reinforce this point with members of my team from time to time when the situation is appropriate. For instance, members of my team will sometimes make it a point to say 'thank you' to me if I eliminate a barrier or help them in some way that they feel is significant. My response is nearly always the same, 'You're welcome. There is no need to thank me; we are a team. We each have a role to play. Together, we will make each other more successful.' I am sure you consider your employees as part of your team. I believe your goal should be to make sure your people consider *you* as part of *their* team.
- **'I could not have achieved this without your support.'** This is quite possibly the highest form of saying 'thank you'. Acknowledging someone else's effort for going above and beyond—especially if it makes a leader or manager look good—reinforces a strong team culture. This simple act of encouragement is a mental booster that will send ripples of trust across the organization.
- **'You're welcome.'** Saying, 'You're welcome' is a proxy for how frequently you assist others. The more you repeat it, the more it becomes a reality. And don't ruin the moment for the other person when you're acknowledged. Don't say, 'It was nothing' or 'I didn't actually do anything.' Simply say, 'You're welcome' or 'I'm glad I could assist/I'm happy to help!'
- **'Well, it wasn't just me, it was the entire team.'** This one's for when outsiders come and ask you during celebration parties or conferences *how* exactly you achieved success in

a particular project. Only talking about yourself while your staff is around, listening to you, will only make you come across as a credit-eater. Why will people work under you if you consume all the praises for *their* work?

Remember, great leaders are humble. Humility, according to studies, provides major leadership benefits such as the ability to listen more effectively, establish better teams and improve work performance. Accepting that you aren't the only cause for your company's success allows you to draw on the wisdom and perspectives of a larger group of people, which typically leads to more effective solutions.

Here Are Some Words Exceptional Leaders Avoid

- 'But…'
- 'I don't have time for this.'
- 'There's nothing I can do about it…'
- 'Just…' (We use 'just' to make tasks seem small and minimize how much time they will take so you can get to 'real work'. Some actually use it so often, it ends up being applied to almost every task they undertake.)
- 'It's *your* fault!'
- 'I'm so disappointed in you.'
- '*Obviously!*'
- 'I think…maybe…could…' (it's just lazy, uncertain language)
- 'None of your business!' (after all, it *is* your team's business, literally and metaphorically)
- 'Pretty…' (diminishes your message and is entirely unnecessary)
- 'Might…' (will you, or won't you? People look to leaders for clarity and accountability.)
- 'I don't take no for an answer.'

- 'I don't know.'
- 'I don't care how…just make it happen!'
- 'Because I'm the one in-charge!'
- 'Are you challenging my authority?'
- 'I need solutions, not problems!'
- 'That's your problem, not mine.'
- 'Failure isn't in *my* dictionary!'
- 'If…' ('If' casts doubt and represents vagueness.)
- 'I'm self-made.' (Nobody's an island. Even so-called 'self-made' leaders need their teams to succeed and survive.)
- 'It is what it is.'
- 'I don't have any feedback for you.'
- 'I achieved that!' (Use, '*we* achieved that' instead and see the difference)
- 'Person A is doing so much better than you.'

Takeaways

- Great leaders are great communicators and orators.
- Great leaders know how to listen effectively and speak.
- Great leaders use positive vocabulary—a strong tone and confident body language to captivate their audience.
- Great leaders also let others share the spotlight by asking questions and taking genuine feedback.
- Great leaders do not use confusing, ambiguous and lazy language; they are clear, concise and alluring with their words.

8

YOU ARE YOUR OWN STATEMENT

> *Your brand is a gateway to your true work. You know you are here to do something—to create something or help others in some way. The question is, how can you set up your life and work so that you can do it? The answer lies in your brand. When you create a compelling brand, you attract people who want the promise of your brand—which you deliver.*
>
> —Dave Buck

Is your image important to you? Are you aware of how your image can impact you and others? In the midst of the Covid-19 crisis, it is more important than ever before, that people—and especially leaders—know what their image and leadership brand are doing for them.

Think about your most recent purchase. Did you choose a particular brand over another? Did you make this choice based on your previous experience with that brand in terms of cost, quality, consistency and ease of use? Maybe the brand fits with your lifestyle or values? Brand acts as a signal to consumers, and in turn, our brand choices reveal part of ourselves to those around us. Think about a company you admire for their leadership.

Amazon, Wal-Mart, Disney, Lexus, Microsoft, American Express, Procter & Gamble and Apple are just a few examples. What do these companies have in common? How did they become known for their ability to lead? Researchers have discovered that firms known for their leadership all have one thing in common: they develop a leadership brand.

Company	Distinguishing Identity of the Company	Leaders in the Company Are Known For
Apple	Innovation and design in technology.	Creating new products and services that break industry norms.
Wal-Mart	Reduced costs of essentials.	Managing costs efficiently; getting things done on time.
Disney	Creativity and customer satisfaction.	Delighting guests with an exceptional and personalized experience.
Procter & Gamble	Innovative self-care products as per consumer needs/demands.	Developing consumer insights, targeted marketing, product innovation.
Lexus	Stylish, luxurious designs of vehicles.	Managing quality processes to improve their high-quality products constantly.

Your personal leadership brand is no different from this. Developing and sharing your leadership brand lets your team and colleagues know who you are, what you stand for and how you work. In the iconic Jeff Bezos's words, 'Your brand is what people say about you when you are not in the room.'

There are many people with good leadership skills and the potential to be powerful leaders. However, most of them do not realize the importance of creating a personal brand for their leadership, and hence, they become invisible. Because they are not 'seen', invisible leaders are unable to acquire the trust of others to make a positive difference. Most people are unaware that you exist if you are not seen. With all of the unnecessary noise, distractions and confusion in today's world, leaders who model or even create a strong leadership brand are able to cut through the clutter and focus all of their efforts on the things that really matter. This is how leaders can genuinely make a difference when they have an authentic, powerful and strong leadership brand.

You could be a leader with tremendous potential and a real passion to make a sustainable difference. However, it's going to be much harder for you to successfully make a difference if others around you are not clear on who you are or do not see your leadership qualities. You must generate awareness, either consciously or unconsciously, in order to maximize your leadership potential. As previously stated, you must be willing to be vulnerable in order to develop trust, inspire respect, and inspire confidence in others so that they can rely on you to follow your path.

A leadership brand raises awareness of what you stand for as a leader and what qualifies you to make a good impact. As Norm Smallwood put it in the *Harvard Business Review*, 'A leadership brand conveys your identity and distinctiveness as a leader. It communicates the value you offer.'[14]

Unlike reputation, which is formed by your past experiences

---

[14] Norm Smallwood, 'Define Your Personal Leadership Brand in Five Steps', *Harvard Business Review*, 29 March 2010, https://hbr.org/2010/03/define-your-personal-leadershi#:~:text=is%20not%20trivial.-,A%20leadership%20brand%20conveys%20your%20identity%20and%20distinctiveness%20as%20a,having%20the%20impact%20it%20could., Accessed on 22 March 2022.

and interactions, your brand is about who you are *now* and how you want to be seen, and that's why it's so important that you have full control over it; it defines your present and future. Personal branding is about taking responsibility over *how* you show yourself. Self-branding can help you build your reputation as a leader if you want to establish yourself as an expert or influencer in your field. You may establish a personal brand that appeals to people all around the world by showing unique character features and maintaining an active online presence.

What do you want to be remembered for as a leader? What do you stand for? What do you believe in? As a leader, you must live your *Values*, create your *Outcomes*, use your *Influence*, be *Courageous* and wrap it all up in your unique *Expression* to find your 'VOICE'. It all comes down to how you communicate your personal brand as a leader to your team, peers and colleagues, clients and community. Develop your communication skills. Make people want to follow you. Bring your skills and abilities to the table. Build and re-invent your own brand to stay renewed and revitalized. You are expressing who you are with your voice by taking that position, stating your opinion, making yourself known and articulating what matters to you. You're demonstrating your leadership abilities.

Developing a strong personal brand to set yourself apart from the competition is a bold move. Leaders must understand that their presence is important in all aspects and will play a key part in their effort to make an impact. A comprehensive personal branding system could be the key to developing a powerful personal leadership brand. This will not only help you get to the next level but also help your team as well.

Developing your leadership brand requires significant investment and a willingness to acknowledge both strengths and weaknesses. Your leadership brand is also a work in progress, changing and evolving as you move through your life and career. So, don't worry about creating a final, defined vision. Developing a personal leadership brand is like scaling Mount Everest. It necessitates attention, commitment and long-term effort—so much effort, in fact, that many people forego making one entirely. (It is their biggest blunder!)

Personal branding is too vital to ignore or get wrong whether you're an entrepreneur or aspiring leader. In today's corporate world, entrepreneurs face stiff competition. This implies you'll need to give your customers a cause to choose you as well as your products. People want to do business with those they like and believe in. So, your personal brand needs to be more likable than your competitor's. Employees want to work with leaders they appreciate and trust—it's basic human psychology.

The best part about building a personal leadership brand is that you gain recognition and are acknowledged as a potential leader, irrespective of your position in the corporate hierarchy. Your power becomes infinite. If you know the right strategies, you can not only gain the right tools, you can even shrink the mountain. Want to gain better tools to climb your Mount Everest? Here you go:

1) **Firstly, identify the right leadership brand for you.** Whether you realize it or not, you already have a personal brand. Your team and colleagues use what you say and do, and what you don't say and don't do, to decide what kind of leader and person you are.

    But do you have the right one that taps and showcases maximum potential? Your leadership brand is comprised of a complicated dynamic, such as how you behave, respond and interact with various groups or individuals in various situations—as well as how you, as a leader, interact with others to achieve amazing results. So, how can you select the best leadership brand for you? Continue reading the next point.

2) **Identify your values.** While selecting a future leadership brand, ask yourself these questions. What would you like to be remembered for? What are your core strengths? What do you stand for, and what do you oppose? What impact did your values play in your life's major accomplishments and failures? What are some of the values you admire in others? In your company, what values do you admire? Make a list of everything you enjoy about your current job, and another list of everything you'd rather not be doing. This level of clarity will aid in the development of your professional goals and the decisions you make to achieve them.

3) **Deconstruct the current brand you've developed unconsciously.** In a nutshell, consider how others see you. Consider how you learn, share information, and influence people. Request input on your communication and decision-making approaches, as well as your strengths and limitations, from your manager, teammates and family. Make a list of popular keywords and areas where you can improve. Once you know what your natural brand is, you can polish it further and align it with your personal-brand goals.

4) **EQ—Emotional Quotient.** A Bain & Company survey of 2,000 employees found that the ability to be mindfully present (called centeredness) was seen as the most important trait among 33 leadership traits.[15] At work, mindfulness

---

[15]Mark Horwitch and Meredith Whipple Callahan, 'How Leaders Inspire: Cracking the Code', Bain & Company, 9 June 2016, https://www.bain.com/insights/how-leaders-inspire-cracking-the-code/, Accessed on 23 March 2022.

can improve emotional intelligence, promote creativity and innovation, and reduce impulsive behaviour. In my experience, empathy and compassion are essential for fostering teams and increasing productivity. Empathy is an important part of emotional intelligence which can help you create trust and rapport with others. An empathetic leader prioritizes the 'why' over the 'what'. Understanding the range and fundamental causes of your emotions, as well as how to use them wisely, can help you understand who you are and how you interact with people more effectively.

5) **Show you have a plan.** Define what success will look like for you in two months, nine months or two years. Leaders are always envisioning a successful future, remember?

6) **Where can you leave a mark?** Your leadership brand must clearly communicate your unique contribution to an organization or project. Think about what impact you currently have and what kind of results you wish to deliver in the next 12 months.

7) **Choose an accountability-pal.** Choose someone who will tell you the truth about how others perceive you. They can also assist you in sticking to your other leadership brand goals. Take feedback from others into account, whether it's from your boss, friends, significant other or co-workers. Does what they say about how others perceive you match your desired image? In order to be more productive, ask your partner what you can do more or less of.

8) **Advertise your brand.** Just the way brands use media to lure customers like me and you to check them out, you have to aim to share your personal brand through social media, networking, outreach and speaking opportunities. Consider social media, blogging, vlogging, podcasts and other ways that you could promote your personal brand in a way that

will showcase your potential as a leader. Blowing your own horn tactfully will get you to places.

9) **Show your executive presence.** A mindful and focused leader *exudes* leadership presence in the workplace. Mindfulness can help people connect emotionally with themselves and others. The ability to stay attentive and present is a crucial aspect of executive presence. The formula is simple: to improve your executive presence and leadership skills, focus on mindful communication. The world right now requires a leader with the gravitas to lead decisively and the compassion to serve with honesty.

- Develop your communication skills. Positive body language, eye contact, proper posture, and active listening can all help you communicate more confidently. Examine how you present yourself. Connect with competence and genuineness.
- Maintain a level of consistency. Leaders who appear to have seamless presence have, ironically, invested in rehearsals, practise sessions, and feedback to polish their leadership brand strategy.

10) **Express yourself (Yes, this is different from communicating).** As important as good communication is, expression is more than just speaking, writing and listening skills. Expression is establishing your personal style as a leader so that people know in an instant what you stand for and how you'll react in a given situation.

Identify your values, vision, purpose and ambitions, then package them into a genuine expression that is both unique and consistent. Define your target audience and craft your essential messages. With whom are you in contact? After that, choose your communication tools. What is the most effective way for you to reach out to your target audience?

Create open and predictable avenues for your teams' ideas, debate and feedback.

11) **Shine in public speaking engagements.** Can you speak confidently and knowledgeably about a subject in your field? If so, you have an advantage that many of your competitors don't. Millionaire entrepreneur Sam Ovens offers the following advice: 'Each media hit, speaking opportunity or social media post has the potential to bring you a new customer. Personal branding is an essential tool for business success.'

Ovens is correct in bringing up the topic of speaking opportunities. They are quite effective at generating consumers for many new entrepreneurs. Speaking allows you to create a brand image as methodically as if you were an artisan building your brand out of clay. You can communicate the energy level you want, your sense of humour and your unique, dynamic passion by creating an image that reflects your preferred style—whether casual, hip or formal.

12) **Include everyone (the more, the merrier, right?)** It's not just about you when it comes to expressing yourself. It's all about the connections you make with your clients, customers, co-workers, team and community. It's all about the personal connections you build and the relevance of your message. It's all about how you hold yourself—your nonverbal communication. It entails explaining your organization's vision, as well as persuading and enlisting others to join you on your journey.

13) **Lastly, *live* your brand.** A brand is a promise, one that you make and fulfil over and over. That's how you develop and solidify it, right? Be true to yourself, understand your strengths and liabilities, and don't try to be *all* things to *all* people.

In *Learning Leadership: The Five Fundamentals of Becoming an Exemplary Leader*, James M. Kouzes and Barry Posner argue that consistency and frequency distinguish adequate and brilliant leaders from ordinary workers.[16] Share your mission statement with your colleagues so they know what to expect from you. A public commitment to your leadership brand makes it difficult for you to abandon your course at the first hurdle and creates a network of supporters.

Basically, if you talk that talk, you better walk that walk.

Make a Statement (Through Your Personal Brand Statement)

One of the first things you need to do when creating your personal brand is to establish a powerful personal branding statement. This short statement will serve as the cornerstone for all of your future branding initiatives, so it's critical to get it properly.

A personal brand statement is a one or two sentence phrase that concisely summarizes what you do and who you are. It's essentially your defining feature, the thing you do better than anyone else. Think of it as your slogan. The most effective personal branding statements are memorable, catchy and attention-getting. Whether you're a job seeker, freelancer or entrepreneur, you should create a personal branding statement. An excellent personal brand statement can help anyone who wants to network and stand out as a prospective leader.

1) **Know your target audience.** So, what type of employer or client can you help most? Large corporations? Growth-

---

[16]James M. Kouzes and Barry Posner, *Learning Leadership: The Five Fundamentals of Becoming an Exemplary Leader,* Wiley, 2016.

stage companies? E-commerce companies? That's the type of phrase you want to use. Talk to them in *their* language.

2) **Keep it short and sweet.** When writing a leadership brand statement, less is more. Some authors cite using one to two sentences. This restricts creativity. I suggest using as many sentences as necessary but keeping your statement to 75 words or less.

3) **Be authentic.** Make use of words that expresses who you are. Use free-flowing dynamic language if you're an entrepreneur. Your language should mirror your evenness if you are steady and paced. Your leadership statement will be more meaningful and credible if you use language that is consistent with your personality. Describe 2-3 essential traits to begin, explain your defining leadership attribute and what it means to you, list 2-3 historical strengths and the results or outcomes you achieved; and finally, list 3-4 passions in short, precise lines to conclude.

4) **Make it unforgettable.** Your statement expresses your personal leadership worth to the rest of the globe. You want it to be eye-catching, especially if you use it as the summary statement on your résumé. You want it to be interesting to read. You want it to captivate your audience. You want it to inspire you. Use wording that stands out. Pose questions, engage in conversation and be amusing!

5) **Show, don't just tell.** Mentioning that you've helped many clients/companies succeed in the past is a great way of showing you'll be able to help the next customer too.

6) **Be inclusive.** We love using the word 'let's', because it shows that you'll be partnering and working towards a common goal. This shows your ability to move with a team as an effective leader or entrepreneur.

Here are some descriptive words you could use to build your personal leadership brand statement:

- Transformation strategist
- Catalyst for future-forward change
- Champion of efficiency and continual improvement
- Charismatic peacemaker
- Transformative go-getter
- Connector: connecting people and resources
- Bringing human beings and ideas together
- Enabler, influencer and motivator
- Problem-identifier, problem-solver *and* problem-preventer
- Leader who establishes solutions in crisis
- Passionate 'go-getter'
- Leader of change inspired by customers
- Brand advocate
- Passionate driver of outstanding design that users love and value
- Innovator who creates winning strategies
- Servant leader and remover of road blocks
- Trend-setter, barrier-breaker and innovation-maker
- Operations data leader
- Key public communicator
- Visionary product leader

Takeaways

- Being a great leader isn't enough. You have to build your brand and show it off. (humbly, of course)
- Your leadership brand makes you visible to other great minds and creates networks helpful for the success of your firm.
- Your leadership brand also makes you visible to other leaders

within the organization, even if you're not too high on the organizational hierarchy.
- Your leadership brand requires you to know your skill-set, strengths and passions.
- Your leadership brand statement defines you and creates an impact. Think of yourself as a product and this statement as a catchy, unforgettable tagline.

9

AUTHORITY VS *TRUE* LEADERSHIP

Remember the difference between a boss and a leader; a boss says 'Go!'—a leader says 'Let's go!'

—George E.M. Kelly, 12th pilot of the
U.S. Army's Aeronautical Division

Throughout my professional life, I have noticed that there are two types of superiors: those you fear and those you respect. Most people mistake fear for respect, but it is different and you can't have both.

Fear is clearly defined as, 'To be afraid of (someone or something) as likely to be dangerous, painful, or threatening.'

The fear-method of leadership, I've always noticed, is less productive and unfortunately, more common nonetheless. Professionals are *constantly* in fear of losing their jobs or getting yelled at for making a mistake. This method also leads to dishonesty, as you cannot truly trust your co-workers in fear, they may be trying to sabotage you in order to gain favours of the manager. It's pretty simple—just like you see in horror movies, fear paralyses you. You can't move away, you can't think straight, and so, boom, you're killed.

Respect, on the other hand, is the less common method

but brings out *brilliant* results. It is also the more difficult road. A respect-based leader willingly listens to the complaints and ideas of their employees and understands that they or their firm cannot always be perfect. A superior who respects their employees does not talk down to them or micromanage them, allows them to have influence on how the company is managed and is prepared to recognize that an employee may know more than they do.

Employees who respect their employer will be harder workers, more loyal and will stick around longer. You already know: fear suffocates, respect motivates. Fear destroys self-confidence, respect builds it. Fear is demanded. Respect is earned. That's exactly the difference between having authority as a boss and having power as a true leader.

There's no scientific formula to compare a leader versus a boss, but think of it this way: being a boss doesn't grant you devotion nor does it inspire those around you. It only grants you the authority to enforce your directions. A good leader, on the other hand, doesn't need that formal power; they simply set the example for people to follow. The power they have over their people is far better as compared to any formal power. And this power stays, *forever.*

Leaders are found in the middle of the effort, working hard, supporting their teammates, solving problems, and shouldering responsibility, whereas bosses give orders and observe. Leaders rise from inside, like a strongman carrying a Volkswagen without an engine, championing the team effort, recognizing exceptional work, and defending the team against critics.

The position of authority is defined by the player's character, while leadership is defined by the player's personality. Authority does not automatically grant you devotion or inspire those around you. It gives you the authority to issue commands, but a smart leader understands that their work entails much more than issuing orders and evaluating the outcomes. After all, how dissimilar does 'bossing a team around' and 'leading a team' sound?

The Key Aspects of Authority

- This is formal power that comes from one's title, role or position within a hierarchy.
- Uses external motivators such as rewards and bonuses.
- Authority ensures the obligatory effort of others, out of fear.
- As authority resides within a position, it may be short-lived and transferable.
- Authority enforces rigid rules, procedures and policies.
- Authority is unidirectional, from the superior to the subordinate.

The Key Aspects of Leadership

- It is the influence and persuasion that comes from one's charismatic personality.
- It triggers internal motivation and confidence in others.
- The role of a leader can be chosen irrespective of one's position in the organization.
- It can be transferred across various employees.
- It creates intangible rewards in others, like personal growth and job contentment.
- It leads to productive conversation among peers, regardless of their position in the organization.

See a clear difference? Let me now demonstrate how a boss is different from a true leader:

The Boss	The Leader
'Boss' is a word that elicits negative reactions. When we say someone is bossy', we usually don't mean they're acting in a particularly good way. Being a boss has a distinct status, and the individual who holds it is in a higher position in the organization than the employees he or she is in charge of. In some ways, being a boss denotes a specific position of power, and regardless of how you feel about it, a boss will have control over his or her subordinates as a result of this role.	'Leader', on the other hand, is a word, which gets a more positive response from people. We tend to say things like 'He was a natural leader' or 'She was a great and accomplished leader.' The association with the word is more positive, and the word is often used only in the context of people we admire and respect.
A boss is a subject matter expert. They have impressive technical skills and experience.	But a great leader is an emotional and people expert. A great leader is very sensitive (but not emotional) which is why they have fantastic strategies for conflict resolution in teams.
A boss, by virtue of his position of power, instructs his employees what to do and expects them to follow through. A boss issues directions and supervises employees, ensuring that those under his or her supervision do their jobs properly.	A great leader is never just a person who instructs and uses power provided by the position. A leader will tell and more importantly, *show* the direction and be a part of the journey to get to the destination. While the focus is still on getting the required jobs done, the emphasis with a leader is not solely on the outcome, but also on the process.

Authority vs True Leadership • 115

For a boss, the end objective is profit. A boss has a responsibility to ensure that the organization achieves the best financial outcomes possible in order to ensure the company's survival. The boss is unconcerned about how his employees go from point A to point B, because the end result is all that matters. If you are able to meet the objectives and do it in a timely manner, the boss will be pleased because you have assured them a profit.	On the other hand, a leader is focused on changing people and the organization. The ideal situation for a leader is to achieve change, a transformation of the organization being A to being B. A true leader is interested in helping their team grow as employees and as people. Instead of placing attention on the outcome, the leader will be more interested in the process and the people behind it.
Bosses need you to perform well for *their* success.	A leader wants you to feel successful even if you failed. They focus on *your* success. One of the incredible characteristics of a leader is linking their success to the successes of those they lead. If those people do not succeed, the leaders have failed in both their minds—and hearts.
A boss holds you accountable.	A leader grows the confidence and passion from within you to build self-accountability.
A boss approaches work in an administrative fashion. The supervisor takes a commanding approach to work, expecting his or her subordinates to obey his or her orders to the letter. A boss would have laid out a strategy and agreed to particular procedures, which he or she expects his or her subordinates to follow.	The approach is rather different with a leader. A leader approaches the work through innovation and collaboration. Since change is the driving force and the vision is the focus of the leader, the approach is to transform and shake things around. It is not about creating the most efficient routines and sticking with the processes that have been proven to work the best. The premise is to find new ways to do things and find new, equally beneficial, routes to the objectives.

One of the biggest delineators being a boss is evoking fear due to authority. A boss depends on positional power to have an impact.	However, leadership influence is not dependent on power or position. Some of the most fantastic leaders you might have encountered at work were the ones who had no authority over the people they influenced.

How Do You Move from Being a Boss to Being a True Leader?

- **Influence, don't command.** A key difference is that a boss's authority comes from their position, whereas a true leader's authority comes from their ability to influence others. Persuade your employees to follow tasks through and explain how they will grow through them rather than thrusting those tasks endlessly on to them. You'll witness what utter devotion feels like.
- **Listen, don't always talk.** To see the whole picture, a leader needs a team of people who bring information forward at the right time. A boss usually sticks to talking to their employees and giving instructions. However, a true leader knows how to observe and listen.

    By creating open conversations, the leader will hear about issues before they become larger problems. This avoids problems, errors and conflicts in the future.
- **Serve, don't see yourself as a God.** A leader sees himself as a servant, not like the boss that sees himself as a God. Leaders frequently identify with their followers and see their position as an opportunity to serve and improve others. Bosses may take a forceful approach to fixing problems or dealing with situations, but a leader can help you understand why you must accomplish a task in a certain way.

- **Don't just explain, inspire.** You shouldn't just explain a task and leave it in your employee's hands. A boss makes sure you understand and do your work, while a leader encourages and guides you. Success necessitates passion. Without a desire to complete tasks, employees will be less motivated to deliver their best efforts. As their boss, you should inspire them by emphasizing the importance of their work.
- **Create a space where your team learns.** Feedback sessions with the boss can create dread in employees, but it doesn't have to be this way. When an employee's course or work needs to be corrected, there is an opportunity for you to show them how to do it better and make them feel valued. By thinking as an advisor rather than a critic, a leader helps move things in a positive direction.

    Your office door should also be open for celebratory sessions, and you should give credit where credit is due. By creating regular, positive feedback cycles, the dread of meeting with a superior can instead become positive anticipation.
- **Don't delegate tasks, delegate authority.** Micromanaging is the sign of a weak boss, and leaders know that the people hired to do the job were hired because they could do the job. Delegating authority to those working for you frees you up to focus on more pressing matters.

    At the same time, when you delegate a new task, it is your responsibility as a leader to ensure that you follow through. Despite your team being skilled, you can't just walk away from the task thinking it's not your problem anymore.

    A boss gets results by telling people what to do and is concerned with doing it correctly, but a leader gets results by empowering their team to figure out what to do and is concerned with doing the right thing.

- **You are a part of the team, not above it.** Stop the whole 'this person always does it better' kind of talk, and include your own self in this philosophy. It does not help anyone's morale in any manner. The objective of being a leader is to encourage and enhance the morale of his followers. Don't think of yourself as superior to your team in any manner, even if you have greater talents or power.

    A boss, unlike a leader, does not take the time to get to know his or her employees. Leaders let go of the hierarchical divide and see their team members as equal contributors, whereas bosses see them as subordinates.

- **Stop the commanding and demanding.** *Influence* and *persuade* **instead.** A boss will give out *all sorts of* commands, both the possible and the impossible, and when these aren't carried out, they pester. You must abandon this attitude if you want to be a leader.

    Instead of declaring, 'I need this work by Friday,' and then striding off like the king of the coast, inquire, 'How quickly can you submit this work?' Alternatively, you may offer, 'Can I have the work submitted on Friday so that I can fulfil the week's deadline?'

    Don't just dose your commands since they don't help; they only make people work under duress, which isn't healthy for them. It's possible that you'll have to justify why something needs to be done. That qualifies you as a true leader.

- **Don't discipline, be a mentor.** Employees are human, and mistakes are to be expected. Who you are, as a superior, has a lot to do with how you deal with mishaps and crisis.

    While bosses are more likely to use a reward-punishment system to discourage poor behaviour, great leaders understand that employees benefit from encouragement and mentorship.

It's important to note the strengths and weaknesses of each employee and mentor them independently. Rather than attacking skill gaps, work to patch them by guiding employees through their shortcomings and building their confidence in new areas.

The Knack of Persuasion

Persuasion typically plays a role in the outcome of any scenario we face in life. You might be trying to persuade a youngster to clean their teeth, urge a friend to go to dinner at a restaurant you enjoy, or convince your repairman to come to your house at a time that is convenient for you. We all practise the art of persuasion, regardless of who we are or what we do.

What do you believe your children are doing when they express their dissatisfaction with you for not purchasing their preferred toys? What are politicians trying to achieve by presenting so much reasoning during an election campaign? Consider a salesperson describing all the advantages of the product he's selling. They're all trying to persuade you and accomplish something with their persuasion skills (i.e., happiness, votes, and sales target).

One of the most important reasons to study about this subject is because persuasion is a major feature of every aspect of human communication. We won't be able to escape it. We won't be able to get rid of it. Persuasion, like Elvis impersonators in Las Vegas, is here to stay.

According to various estimates, the average person is exposed to 300 to 3,000 texts every day. Persuasion is ingrained in our daily encounters with friends, family and co-workers as part of the 'people professions'. There are more ways to persuade than ever before. You can give a TED talk to promote your big idea, engage in hashtag activism, advocating a cause by tweeting or promote change through a website.

In the corporate world, persuasion is used on a daily basis. Consider this: even advertising is a sort of persuasion, in that it tries to persuade clients to come to your store or utilize your services. Persuasion is also important in any negotiation, and for businesses, this could mean persuading vendors to offer better pricing or services. Consider how you deal with employees: you're constantly trying to encourage them to put in more effort, take on new responsibilities, or adjust to workplace changes. Giving orders will not result in employee engagement and dedication. This can only be done through persuasion. Nothing can achieve this better than when you motivate your workforce to embrace your vision and goal for the organization. Hence, the need to learn the art of persuasion. It is not only necessary for employees to know how to persuade their bosses but also crucial for executives to influence their workforce.

US President, Lyndon Johnson famously said, 'The only real power available to the leader is the power of persuasion.' He wasn't wrong. Success, as a leader, hinges on learning to persuade people at work to buy into your plans and take actions you want them to take without making them want to murder you, basically. How else are you going to keep a team of diverse personalities and opinions on the same page and united?

The age-old anecdote, 'You can catch more flies with honey than you can with vinegar' suggests (correctly, if I may add), that one is likely to achieve better results by persuading and influencing than demanding or commanding.

Leadership and power in twenty-first century firms are dispersed over many partners. Younger generations have a desire for greater meaning and involvement in their firms and are likely to choose soft leaders rather than authoritative ones. The power of a polite 'could you' or 'please' is so much more, than commanding, yelling or ranting.

Today's generationally diverse workplace is a mix of baby boomers, millennials, and Gen X employees. Younger workers are technologically sophisticated, and they're global thinkers. They tend to want to know more than simply what they're expected to do and how to do it. They also want to know *why* they should do it. Modern leaders need to answer such 'why' questions to help people better understand and be more engaged with their roles and with the organization. This is where emotional appeal and persuasion comes into play while leading a team or a project.

What are the benefits of being a persuasive leader, you ask? I got you:

- Lesser confusions in decision-making. This leads to increased efficiency and productivity.
- Quicker problem-solving and conflict-resolution.
- Having your way while making others feel like they're having theirs.
- Better collaboration and teamwork.
- An engaged, passionate and closely-knit team.
- Healthy employee relations and work culture.
- Healthy relations between you and your employees.
- Your team willingly and happily accepts responsibilities.

I don't know if you already know this, but the communicating a leader does is all persuasion, essentially. That's what leaders do. They persuade people to work together, to achieve more than they ever thought they could, to reach for apparently impossible goals and to put personal interests aside (at least temporarily)— in favour of some larger group purpose. What are some ways you master the knack of persuasion, have your way as a leader while also keeping your team happy?

- **First, see if *you* can be persuaded.** To start improving your persuasion skills in leadership, conduct a little self-evaluation on your track record of open-mindedness. If your workplace reputation is for keeping an open mind, being willing to compromise and prioritizing win-win solutions, you're already doing great. Remember, everything in life is a give and take. If you expect that others will always be willing to be persuaded by you, you have to let them persuade you at times too.
- **Establish credibility.** There are two sources of leadership credibility—strong knowledge and strong relationships. There's no substitute for expertise; so, become an expert in your field. Foster a workplace culture of mutual respect for each other and of valuing each other's contributions of ideas.
- **Show empathy to appeal to their emotions.** To be a powerful persuader, understand a person's pain and problems. Try to put yourself in the other person's shoes. Doing this will help you better understand the other person's situation, feelings and motives. If you've had a similar experience, share it. Showing empathy fosters connections and builds trust.

    Research has shown that your emotions contribute to the decision-making process: how people feel about things contributes to how they make decisions. The emotions you elicit in people will either work for or against you. If people feel uncertain about your ideas, then they are likely to vote against them. If they feel emotionally drawn towards you, there's no way you will not persuade them.
- **Show your employees you care.** You might think you're showing interest in your team and colleagues by making

small talk and asking how their weekend was, but is it coming across as genuine care? Being authentic and going beyond surface-level conversation shows that you actually care what they have to say. If someone knows you care about them deeper than just a co-worker relationship, they'll go above and beyond to help you.
- **Ask and hear them out.** The best persuaders are innately curious about the world around them and the people with whom they interact. Learn what others need on a physical as well as emotional level and why. Always ask good questions and then listen. Begin open-ended discussions that start with, 'Tell me…' Demonstrate a genuine interest in others and get to know their desires, dreams and goals. Once you understand a person's position, you'll be better equipped to persuade him.
- **Know their background.** Learning about the background information of your client, co-workers, employees or boss helps you to get a better understanding of how they think and communicate. Finding out background information is not about digging into another person's private life. What you want to find out is how any previous experience, exposure and education would impact how that person receives your information.

  Armed with this knowledge, you would aim to ensure they would have a positive experience, and you would present your ideas in a way that you alleviate the fear of them thinking they would have the same negative experience.
- **Everyone loves a win-win.** Nobody wants a deal or an idea that won't benefit them. It is not enough for you to think you are presenting a win-win proposal, you must also *show* them that your idea would be good for them as well. Present your opinion in a way people can easily see what's in it for

them. Find out what their goal is and connect your ideas to how it can help them achieve those goals. Help them connect the dots. It is your responsibility to show them the value your proposition has for them.
- ***And* great stories.** There's nothing quite as compelling or fascinating as a story well told. Even children love a good story. Stories have the power to persuade others and influence them. People may pay attention differently when hearing a narrative as opposed to just facts and figures. If you want to demonstrate why an idea or strategy is important, then tell a well-crafted story. Your stories must create connections between what the person is thinking, what he already believes and what you want him to believe and do.
- **Paint a pretty picture.** Employees like to know how their role, no matter how small, is having an impact and furthering the company's big goals. To this end, Sara Bonham, co-founder of Perennial, advises leaders to bring everything back to the mission of a business. 'Paint a much larger picture of why this company was created and how innovation is first thought of,' says Bonham. 'Once people are sold on this, they will support the granular, tactical day-to-day work, as they know everyone is working toward a common goal.'[17]

Here's an Example of the Subtle Art of Persuasion for You

- The group of college students had agreed on the ideal type of person, and there were two obvious candidates within the group, Jessica and Rob.

---

[17]Young Entrepreneur Council, '8 Strategies for Becoming a More Persuasive Leader', *Inc.*, https://www.inc.com/young-entrepreneur-council/8-strategies-for-becoming-a-more-persuasive-leader.html, Accessed on 23 March 2022.

- Jessica suggested that Rob should take on the task. Rob knew he couldn't handle extra work due to his job but said 'yes' happily since he wanted the power.
- Decision made. Everyone smiled, except for one member of the group, Steve.
- Steve, who had until that moment been silent, said: 'Rob, don't forget to let us know what you want us to do to help. With your new job, you're going to have a lot on, and you'll need to make sure you get us organized or we won't get it all done.'
- All the members nodded their heads and looked at Rob empathetically. 'We know you have the skills Rob, and we need you on the team. However, we don't want you feeling burnt-out.' Steve added.
- 'You know, on consideration, I'm not sure I've got time to complete this, let alone start my new job,' Rob stated thoughtfully. 'As you say, I've had a lot going on. It might be best if Jessica took care of it.'
- Everyone stared at Jessica, who responded that if the group wished, she would take it on. They all agreed that was the greatest option.
- Jessica afterwards asked Steve, in private, why he intervened when the group had already chosen a leader. He stated that he believed she would do better than Rob and get a better outcome for the group. He also stated that he did not want Rob to feel overburdened or overworked.
- In this scenario, Steve had gently used his persuasion abilities to get what he wanted, resulting in a win-win situation out of an otherwise uncomfortable meeting. Without knocking Rob down in any way, he persuaded the group to choose Jessica as the leader.

- Rob was pleased that the group had recognized his abilities and initially picked him, and he was equally pleased, even if he wasn't in charge of the assignment, because Steve made him feel cared for by his entire team.
- At the end, Steve had always wanted Jessica to lead the project, and he achieved so, without him ever having to risk upsetting Rob by saying that he thought Jessica would be better.
- Everyone's happy. See? That's classic persuasion for you.

Takeaways

- Modern leadership is based on respect rather than evoking fear out of your team or workers.
- True leadership does not oppress; rather, it persuades and influences.
- Your persuasion as a leader lets you have your way, while also making your team members think they're having theirs.
- Persuasion has a lot to do with how things are said when, where and to whom. Know the other party well.
- Persuasion has a lot to do with verbal softeners and emotional appeal.

10

HAVE A SAY, SWAY THEM AWAY

Leadership is influence. It is the ability to obtain followers. When the leaders lack confidence, the followers have no commitment. A leader is great not because of his power, but because his ability to empower others.

—John C. Maxwell

Persuasion is the process of persuading someone to believe or do something. Influence, on the other hand, is the power to affect someone else's way of thinking. Persuasion and influence can both be used to motivate people, therefore both concepts have important connotations for someone who wishes to be a successful leader. They are motivational techniques in this context.

However, many people make the mistake of thinking that persuasion and influence are the same thing. That, buddy, is far from the truth. Yes, they are both a means to an end, and many times, they involve swaying opinions. But there is one thing that influence has and uses that persuasion does not use, and that is your reputation.

Persuasion can be used to get someone to do something or make a decision without having to gain their trust. When it comes to influencing others, taking the effort to win their trust is essential to motivating them to act or make a specific decision.

When used indiscriminately, persuasion might easily be equated to the capacity to 'sell ice to Eskimos'. But, if the Eskimos learn you've sold them something they don't actually need, will they trust you or buy from you again?

Even if it's only a few minutes later, how confident are you in your decision? There's a good chance you have reservations. You have reservations or 'buyer's remorse' since you don't necessarily trust the person who persuaded you. On the other hand, a strong leader who takes the time to reduce any uncertainty before encouraging others to act or make a decision can use persuasion techniques without coming across as a manipulative fool. Basically, persuasion doesn't work in the long run without influence. If persuasion is the hammer you pull out the moment you see a nail, influence is the apprenticeship and training you go through to become a carpenter.

Influence develops as a result of well-nurtured relationships. It's the end-result of a series of actions, behaviours and intents aimed at establishing credibility, developing trust and adding value. Persuasion may be a more 'in the moment' talent. It takes a unique blend of charisma, talent and technique to get things done quickly and effectively. Surprisingly, despite its use, persuasion is best received by those who believe in the persuader's level of influence. In general, you can't persuade without having power.

Persuasion usually becomes a deliberate attempt where the persuader wishes to alter the course of action of the individual through communication. Reasoning with the individual is one such technique. If you are successful, persuasion is said to have been at work. Some great leaders and orators have the power of the chatter. They are great orators and can sway the opinion and behaviour of others easily.

Influence is larger than persuasion. Whenever there is a change in a person's thoughts, feelings or behaviour because of another person's personality, then influence is said to have taken place. Great leaders have this ability or charisma to make others behave or do what they want without actually saying it in words.

Both influence and persuasion have the common objective of making a change in a person's behaviour or attitude, whereas persuasion requires you to communicate, influence works silently without you having to make any effort.

I mean that anyone can persuade another person with some slick graphics and fancy words. But when you're working on changing minds through influence, it is likely that the people you're working with are people who know you, or at least, they know your reputation. Influence involves trust and a relationship, where persuasion deals more with communication, solid facts and figures—which are manipulated to get the desired outcome. When it comes to influence, your reputation is your best asset.

Successful leaders are highly effective influencers. In fact, the ability to influence people—to motivate, energize and direct them in the quest for strategic goals—is so integral to the definition of leadership as to be virtually synonymous with it.

For example, business is a time sensitive environment. You do not have an eternity to get your employees or team members motivated to achieve a common objective. Though persuasion is a handy technique in any circumstance, influence is preferred by most leaders as it is based upon trust and credibility, which are lacking in persuasion. For example, it is possible to sell combs to bald men through persuasive techniques. However, they will feel cheated when they realize that combs are of no use to them and that you have sold them what they do not need. Suddenly, all the trust for a person who persuaded is gone. In contrast, attitude and behavioural change that results because of influence is longer and has better results. In the presence of trust, both influence and persuasion work satisfactorily.

Ways to Influence and Always Have Your Say

- **Polite requests.** Requesting allows you to gain the commitment of the people you lead by making a direct statement of what you want, in a polite manner. Requesting also includes the use of frequent checking and persistent reminders to get people to follow through with their tasks. Making a polite request for a task to be done is just the simplest way to make a demand in a non-threatening way, leaving no room for negotiation but also not suggesting punishment or other bad consequences.

- 'If you could inform Rose that….it would be helpful.'
- 'Could you please call April and…?'
- 'I'd asked you to talk to Chad. Were you able to find the time to do it?'
- 'Could you get me the papers…?'

- **Wear your integrity on your sleeve.** Nothing can ruin your influence and respect faster than a lack of integrity. Influence is something that has to be acquired with honesty and integrity. Influential people understand that they will be held up as an example for others to follow. They act and interact in a genuine and believable manner, and they recognize that their reputation is the cornerstone of their capacity to influence and lead. You'll inspire others to adopt your ideas and support your vision if you're constantly trustworthy and honest in your dealings. Influence and respect come by doing what you say you'll do and following through

on your promises. You must be seen as reliable, sincere, genuine and thoughtful.
- **Give and receive trust.** Give trust so you can earn trust. Experienced leaders understand that the easiest approach to determine whether or not you can trust someone is to do so first. Trust is the glue that keeps all relationships together, and it is the foundational principle of leadership. Teamwork fosters trust, which in turn, promotes progress.
- **Get your hands dirty.** Employees expect a good leader to get their hands dirty and help out when things get tough. Get on the front lines and help out when it's most needed if you want to be persuasive. Make sure you're willing to pitch in and help your team when they need it, and you can rest assured that they'll back you up during the decision-making process.
- **Fulfil their desires.** Help people. Be a resource, a sounding board, a safe place to talk. If you want the people you lead to respect you, they need to know you are on *their* side. Advocate for them; help them get the promotion they've been hoping for. Use your influence for their benefits and see the magic.
- **Know what you're saying.** They are serious about what they say. Influential people avoid gossip and baseless personal attacks on others. They aspire to be more than petty. To gain influence, you must establish clear and simple communications and ensure that your ideas are effectively communicated.
- **But don't be an all-talk-and-no-show.** Match your words with your actions and do what you have promised to do. Basically, practise what you preach.

Also, influential leaders aren't afraid of taking risks or making decisions. They don't allow themselves to become stuck or paralyzed by any emergency. They take action, move forward and find a way around roadblocks. They think before they speak, but they don't hesitate to jump in when necessary. Even when they're acting spontaneously, they're thinking strategically—ensuring they have a plan of action even in the midst of challenges and change.

- **Establish expertise.** Let's face it: nobody's going to listen to you if they realize that you are 'guessing' around something or if you do not show confidence in your ideas or knowledge.

  Although some people try to influence based on their impressions around a topic, without knowledge, they are not able to go deeper into anything. We don't want that, do we?

  It's always easier to influence an audience if people trust you. Many times, the reputation will precede you and people will have already an opinion before they have met you. If they have a good opinion, you've won almost 75 per cent of the battle.

  However, even with a great reputation, you must demonstrate competency in the topic. You should be prepared to focus on what is relevant and be updated around the new trends when presenting an idea or selling a project.

- **Explain your orders.** Explain *why* you want something to be done. You can gently use authority or your expertise to explain and influence. One example is when your boss shows that what they want from you is consistent with policy, procedure or company culture. This makes you appear well-versed with the company's rules and policies and also makes the employee realize the value and urgency of a task.

- 'According to our company's policy, all employees are to....'
- 'As you know, it's a standard practise to...'
- 'Our CEO had asked me to look into the team's progress...'

- **Tag-team.** You can get others on your team to help you extend influence or reach goals you could not accomplish on their own. Create a network of supporters to extend your power-base, build consensus, or you could even create an 'us-versus-them' situation. Leaders who cite the names of their supporters when they make a request make it seem more agreed upon, and hence, important.

> - 'Both Sean and I think that....'
> - 'Everyone on the marketing team suggests we...'
> - 'As a team, we've decided that...'
> - 'I believe everyone agrees it's a good idea to...'

- **Connect with subordinates.** Truly connect with your people. Leaders are responsible for connecting with their people and relating to them in a way that increases their own influence. When you can connect with people, you can begin to form relationships—and relationships are the core foundation of influence.
- **Expect greatness from both yourself *and* your team.** Influential leaders have relentless enthusiasm that drives those around them to accomplish amazing things and to stretch themselves beyond their comfort zones. They encourage others to rise to the challenge and confront obstacles. They understand that failure is possible, but at the same time, they recognize that success won't happen if they don't try. When your employees know you expect great things out of them, they felt acknowledged and know you hold them in high regard.
- **Be present and proactive.** Not only must you be accessible in your office, you must also be proactive with your employees and actively seek opportunities to support their efforts. An

influential leader is accountable to the people he or she manages. Building confidence in management-employee relationships requires accessibility. Get out of the office and away from the desk. Take a walk around the floor and pay attention to the people that work there. Greet them kindly and ask them how their progress is. Someone needs assistance? Be there for them, determine their roadblocks and commit to solving problems and setbacks.

- **Be a social butterfly.** With socializing, leaders start to take an interest in those they are trying to lead. It is okay to use praise and appreciation before/during an attempt to get others to carry out a request or support a proposal. You establish a basis for asking and behaving in a warm and cordial manner to influence others to act, ask friendly questions and disclosing personal information to create a space of intimacy, and bingo, they trust you more.

> - 'I'm in awe of what you have achieved, takes a lot of commitment and dedication. It would be great if you could…'
> - 'I believe so too…'
> - 'My daughter's age is the same as yours…'
> - 'I have been to Germany for a conference too. Beautiful place, isn't it?'
> - 'How are the wife and kids?'

Try to build rapport with people around you by identifying commonalities and matching behaviours/interests or ambitions. We've all learnt this, people are more easily persuaded by those they like.

- **Work on your network.** You can be competent, develop expertise and tell great stories, but through a good network, you will be able to influence others more frequently and without difficulty.

When you have a strong network, your network *endorses* you, which will make people trust you and your capabilities easier. They could open doors and assist you to achieve the final goal.

Also remember, a network is *always* a two-way road. It is not only about what you can get from others, but also what you can give. And do not underestimate your capacity, you will always have something to share and offer to people around you.

- **Swallow your pride.** Leaders recognize that no success is achieved alone. While acknowledgment of others is important, leaders who consistently exhibit gratitude and humility encourage others to act. You inspire more focused, deliberate work from committed employees when you accept your inability to operate alone while showing appreciation and humility for those doing the work. Humility demonstrates that no matter how experienced you may be, you recognize that improvements are always possible.
- **Make it personal.** Personal appeals are more focused on other people, as they assume some form of relationship and trust between a leader and those being influenced. With personal appeals, the leader asks for a personal favour before revealing what it is, such as carrying out a request or supporting a plan out of friendship. A personal appeal entails requesting something based on friendship, loyalty, trust, or a previous relationship. Leaders who use personal appeals may inform their employees that they rely on them.

> - 'You and I go back a long time in this company, Mathew. You're someone I can trust. I'd really appreciate if you could….'
> - 'I don't think I can do this alone. Can you help me?'
> - 'Can I count on you to…?'
> - 'We've both seen this crisis before in the firm, too. Could we work this out together?'

- **Inspire.** Inspiration is the core ingredient of being an influential leader. Understanding others' perspectives and focusing on what lies deep in other people's mind-sets, i.e., their values and emotions and then engaging with them accordingly, inspires the maximum passion and productivity out of them. Appeal to someone's values and ideals or arouse their emotions, and see how you gain commitment for your request or proposal.

> - 'Because you care for the development of children, I'd like you to take on the elementary education project, Anthony.'
> - 'You are the first person I thought of for this task, considering you feel so passionately towards coding, Ashley.'
> - 'Kevin, I remember you telling me you love reading. I finally found a perfect project for you.'
> - 'You're the best one to handle this negotiation, Anne, because you care about being both business-like and environmentally sensitive.'

Encouragement and positivity make you addictive. Influential people convey optimism. They see possibilities and opportunities that others miss. We are inspired by them because we aspire to be like them. They motivate us to do the right thing, to be the best we can be, and to continue pushing boundaries.

You must push yourself and others to perform the seemingly impossible in order to be influential. You must take on the difficult task or project that appears to be overwhelming, but that will be incredibly rewarding and significant if you succeed. As a powerful leader, you have the potential to influence others to change. Ensure that it is for the best.

Takeaways

- Persuasion has more to do with on-the-spot communication, whereas influence happens through a leader's personality and is more long-lasting.
- Your persuasion means nothing if you do not have influence over your team.
- An influential leader charms through their honesty, integrity, wit, encouragement and intelligence.
- An influential leader is the best at leading by example; how they behave becomes how their organization behaves.

11

LEADING FUTURE LEADERS

Great leaders create more leaders: Good leaders have vision and inspire others to help them turn vision into reality. Great leaders create more leaders, not followers. Great leaders have vision, share vision, and inspire others to create their own.[18]

—Roy T. Bennett

'I am the leader, get in line behind me.' This is a dumb rule that has spread like wildfire and developed an inaccurate representation of leadership across the entire business world.

We've all heard the old phrase, 'There's no *I* in team.' Working together, every employee is a valuable asset to the team. This aphorism is followed by a good leader. A great leader, on the other hand, instils in his or her entire team the belief that 'there is no I in team' and prepares them to be future leaders by encouraging leadership in the workplace.

In the professional sphere, there is a lot of discussion about leadership. Very often, I find these discussions are really about how to lead followers. Very rarely, in my own experience, are

---

[18]Roy T. Bennett, *The Light in the Heart*, 2016.

these discussions about the skills required to create new leaders—which is unfortunate because that is where transformational business growth really comes from.

My friend Kyle recently told me he had a chance to work again with a client that he had worked with several years ago. In Kyle's first engagement with that client, he had hired a new leadership team. From their work together at the time, Kyle's initial assessment was that some team members were strong, others were not, and that, over time, the weak ones would be weeded out.

Boy, was Kyle wrong. The weak ones were still there and a number of the strong ones have disappeared. The biggest surprise was that one of the strongest leaders from that initial team was now as weak as the remainders. What happened?

Simple. The poorly led budding leaders, with potential to take over bigger projects, will choose one of two doors: they will leave, or they will become weaker in order to survive—if they are merely treated as followers and their leadership potential isn't tapped. If you treat leaders like followers, they will never gain the independence, strength, or personal accountability they require. Leaders will seek opportunities elsewhere if they are not given the training and opportunities to put what they have learned into practise.

A bridge is only as strong as the foundation that supports it, i.e., a leader is only as strong as the budding leaders standing like pillars behind them whenever they need aid or need to delegate. Don't make nascent leaders stand in line for the chance to demonstrate their growing abilities either. They learn best by putting what they have been studying into practise when they take charge of projects or teams. They, in turn, relish leadership development, because it happens to help them further their careers too.

Understand, followers are dependent—they need to be told what to do. Creating followers bring additional workload for the leader and the exceptional leader understands that very well.

This creates a pattern of dependency that leads to stagnation, as the organization's capacity to change reduces to the capacity of the *single* leader. The poor leader becomes a bottleneck. You cannot expect them to carry the entire organization on their back, can you?

When times are stable, creating followers can make sense. It aligns everyone behind the leader's single goal. But when times are churning (as they have been, ever since Covid-19), the ability to flex and adapt becomes paramount. Leaders who create more leaders increase the capacity of the organization to change and grow. They increase its resilience and agility. Leaders who create more leaders expand their ability to create results at a distance. They increase their own capacity as individuals and the results they are able to achieve; and they increase the ability of their organization to succeed.

Business owners can't just sit back and wait for fully developed new leaders to appear. Employees with leadership potential must be actively identified, and strategies to nurture and develop such potential must be found. Talent development necessitates a significant investment of both time and resources. Think you don't have time? As experienced and polished workers begin to retire or exit, the business loses critical knowledge, and most businesses need to fill vacancies quickly rather than hobble along during a lengthy outside search to find new leaders. No matter how busy you are in the here and now, you've got to spend time each day grooming those team members who will lead your company in the future.

- Creating new leaders prepares them better for future leadership responsibilities or handling tasks when you aren't around. Face it, you cannot be everywhere.
- Fostering budding leaders retains talent and keeps them satisfied.
- Adaptability and change management become easier and more successful.
- Nurturing budding leaders enables efficient and effective delegation.
- It also improves employee engagement.
- You create a high-performing team not always waiting on you for approval or spoon-feeding. A win for them, a win for you.
- More innovation and creativity at the workplace as leaders are always visionaries.
- Improved business lifespan.
- Divided pressure, stress and tasks as you can trust these budding leaders with many tasks. No micromanagement needed.

It may come as a surprise, but your company's next extraordinary leader is probably already right there in your building. It's true, the most successful leaders are those that cultivate leadership from within, even in their subordinates. Why? Because current employees with leadership potential are already familiar with your organization's chain of command, processes, software and systems. They've already proved they are a good fit for the company culture, and they likely already know the organization's strengths and weaknesses (and may even have ideas about how to address these areas of opportunity).

Leadership is not a rank, a title or a position that you must have first dibs on! Leadership is a state of mind in which one's actions motivate others to dream bigger, study more, do more, and grow. You don't have to be a CEO to be a great leader; you only have to be the CIO, or Chief Inspiration Officer, who motivates others to dream, achieve, and lead.

Begin your search for leadership potential by recognizing that leadership potential is easy to spot. These are the employees who are proactive, dependable, and thoughtful in their work, and who somehow manage to take command when necessary. Don't limit your search to persons with degrees. Your future leaders are the employees others go to for help and who others continuously rely upon. Say accounting clerk Madge displays initiative, accuracy and a good facility for numbers, but only has an associate's degree. What can you do to develop her into an accounting department leader, and one day, maybe even the CFO?

So, how exactly do you spot budding leaders?

1) **Be hawk-eyed.** Before you can nurture potential leaders, you must first be able to recognize who they are. Don't just look at performance, look for potential. Yes, leadership requires a high level of performance. A leader, after all, must be capable and knowledgeable. However, not all top performers are suited for leadership jobs, thus performance cannot be the sole criterion. Look for someone who has a high level of motivation and perseverance. Someone who doesn't give up easily, strives for improvement and has an aptitude for teaching others. Seek out people with high emotional intelligence—that is, employees who are able to control their emotions and respond to the emotions of other employees. People with empathy, and those whom others trust and seek out for advice.

2) **Hear how they talk.** One way to spot the natural leaders

within your organization is to pay attention to how they communicate with their colleagues. Is there one person that people often go to for advice or assistance? They could be pointing you towards a potential leader. It is also worth observing how people communicate within meetings, noting how they have prepared for the meeting and how actively they participate in discussion and follow-up actions.

3) **See how they handle their emotions.** How do they perform under stress, short timelines and complexity? Do they try to keep their cool and stay solution-focused and forward-looking? Natural leaders try to give others a sense of clarity or security amid uncertainty.

4) **Hear how they interact with the team.** Do they make an effort to include everyone, to find common ground and to promote peace and understanding? Are they employing language that brings people together or that divides them? Do they appear to be aware of their surroundings, knowing when to challenge and when to back off? Natural leaders are adept at navigating the unseen and attempting to alleviate high-stress situations.

5) **Do they invest in your firm's future?** High-potential leaders will display a high degree of interest in company goals and engage in its future plans and strategy. They are 'all in' and are invested in the future. In assessing these high-potentials, ask these questions, 'Does this employee proactively contribute good ideas and propose strategies for improving the workplace, growing the business, or streamlining a process? Does she show interest in going above and beyond to get results on behalf of the team or the organization?' If you answered 'yes', chances are, you've identified an employee with the makings of a future leader.

6) **How much do they understand their team?** How do

they interact with other people (peers, subordinates, line managers, skip-level managers and stakeholders)? Do they perceive things from a variety of angles? Do they recognize and appeal to various personalities and motivations? Are they valuing the team's benefits rather than simply their own? Natural leaders not only perceive various needs but also coach or mentor others in order to assist them in obtaining what they require. Do they help and guide teammates when they need it?

7) **Do their values align with your company's?** When you're reviewing future leaders for your business, you want to be safe with the knowledge that they share the same core values as your organization and are passionate about what you're trying to achieve. *Forbes* says that, 'By communicating the organization's values and your own, you provide clarity around the why of your decisions and leadership style.'[19] When looking for leadership potential, look for those people who are in tune with, and keen to promote, the company's ethos and values, as this is likely to suggest a reflection of their own personal values.

8) **Can they take up challenges?** Employees can be divided into two groups: those who like to follow orders and those who want to make their own decisions. The former waits for orders before doing, but the latter inspires others to take action. Take note of which employees go above and beyond their job responsibilities on a regular basis or are ready to offer advice on a problem. Give them an impromptu task with a tight deadline, and watch how they respond and

---

[19] Carley Sime, 'The Power Of Values In Leadership', *Forbes,* 15 February 2019, https://www.forbes.com/sites/carleysime/2019/02/15/the-power-of-values-in-leadership/?sh=6687f8e26f76, Accessed on 24 March 2022.

meet the goal. Because leaders must be able to act quickly and decisively, an action-oriented person who can perform well under pressure and make quick, calculated decisions is a promising leader.

9) **Can they handle not being able to complete those challenges?** One of the key skills to identify in potential leaders is the ability to deal with, and recover from, setbacks. This skill relates to high emotional intelligence, which helps people to understand that others are judging them on not just the failure but also on how they handle the failure. Good leaders will show themselves to be accountable in both the good and bad times. So, this is definitely a worthwhile area to pay attention to. Inspiring's managing director, John Telfer comments: 'It's important that leaders and managers are not afraid to show their own weakness by asking for support where needed, especially when new to the role. It's often the case that they will have to learn to cope with managing a team and dealing with all the issues that come with it, whilst continuing to perform their own important role in the company.'[20]

10) **Can they multi-task?** From project management to client services, internal communication to employee development, leaders must be capable of juggling many different tasks at once. Groom your potential leaders by adding more responsibility to their workload. Give them activities that encourage them to develop new abilities and push them beyond their comfort zones. Those who easily absorb new and difficult duties are natural self-starters, a characteristic

---

[20]'How to Identify Future Leaders in Your Organization', Inspiring, 8 July 2021, https://www.inspiring.uk.com/how-to-identify-future-leaders-in-your-organization/, Accessed on 24 March 2022.

that can neither be taught nor is lacking in leadership.

11) **Do they understand their setbacks?** Are they willing to learn from others and change their position when new information emerges? Natural leaders recognize how much they don't know.

12) **Do you see their fire to achieve?** Author and influencer Daniel Goleman says you should look for leaders who are driven to achieve beyond expectations—their own and everyone else's. The first sign is a passion for the work itself. Such people, says Goleman, '...seek out creative challenges, love to learn, and take great pride in a job well done. They also display an unflagging energy to do things better. They are also eager to explore new approaches to their work.'[21]

13) **What does their backstory say?** Looking at an employee's work history is just as important as their current performance. It will help decision makers better ascertain whether, early on, a high-potential employee has demonstrated good leadership.

Retain and Nurture Prospective Leaders

Once you've spotted budding leaders in your organization, retain and nurture them by:

- **Respecting them, first and foremost.** A word to the wise: treat your employees with respect, because if you do, they'll stick with you through thick and thin.
- **Increasing their responsibilities.** Providing opportunities to take on additional responsibility will show your employee

---

[21] Daniel Goleman, 'Traits of a Motivated Leader', LinkedIn, 13 April 2014, https://bit.ly/3uo8LIx, Accessed on 24 March 2022.

how much you trust them. How you do this depends on the person's role and your organization but there are usually ways to offer small leadership roles—such as a place on a committee or chairing a team meeting.
- **Nourishing them *financially* (if you know what I mean).** You might think to yourself, 'Oh no, not salaries and benefits again!' As much as it might sound cliché, offering your employees a nice paycheck and a number of creative benefits can help you in your efforts to keep them at the company. These creative benefits could also include: flexible working hours, gym memberships, free meals, mentoring/development programmes or even remote work opportunities.
- **Giving them exposure.** Ensure that your future leaders are able to fully appreciate all aspects of your business—not just their current department. You should also encourage them to gain a broad understanding of your industry, as well as the future possible directions for your organization. This is essential knowledge for any future business manager who may one day make the decisions that shape your organization.
- **Giving them some good old support.** As an employer, you have a responsibility to support all your employees and your future leaders who will depend on you for support while they further their careers. Not all the decisions they make will be your ideal course of action, yet outwardly showing support for your future leaders demonstrates trust and respect in them.
- **Challenging them with real-life business situations.** Placing your future leaders in real-world business settings will push and strain them to their limits as they try to solve or overcome the problems you set before them. When presented

with unfamiliar activities, giving children challenging or heavy projects will show their strengths and capacities, as well as enhance their critical thinking skills and creativity. They'll gain new talents, and you'll increase their devotion to your business by increasing their confidence in their own abilities.

- **Mentoring and coaching.** Aspiring leaders should feel that there is someone they can turn to for advice, guidance and support on a professional level. You can pick mentors by selecting current leaders, or you can seek advice from retired executives or relevant professionals from other companies. It's critical to create a structured mentorship program, so you can track mentoring progress and determine the specifics of the relationships.
- **Sharpening their soft skills.** One of the biggest challenges you will have, in terms of leadership, has to do with people and the ability to lead them. They may have great management skills, but that doesn't mean they can effectively lead others. In fact, it's a low percentage of people who naturally have the people skill trifecta: the ability to lead, manage and coach others. Sure, performance is an indicator of skill and competence and is required to identify a leader, but you also need to consider an employee's desire and aptitude to grow, develop others, create a vision, communicate effectively, lead a team, and impact all levels of the business. Proceed with caution, and always give more weight to potential than performance on the leadership scale. What you'll find is that some of your employees will show high performance, but they just aren't cut out to be leaders, as much as they'd like to be in that role.
- **Showering them with rewards.** Recognize and praise your future leaders' achievements and growth throughout the

leadership development program. Performance goals, the challenge of increased responsibility, a new job title, cash incentives, or even a greater stake in the company's future or the company itself can all be used to motivate employees. Be sure you know what motivates them and tailor your reward system accordingly. However you reward them, your future leaders will appreciate the gestures and feel more motivated and committed to sharing in the vision of your organization. And remember, as a leader yourself, your management team will look to you for as an example to follow and for best practise. Review your own approach from time to time to ensure you lead by example, and give your future leaders the role model they need.

- **Promoting leaps of faith.** Failures can be costly, so its little wonder many budding leaders avoid taking risks. Ironically, risk intolerance often ends up costing employers more. According to Bersin by Deloitte research, organizations whose culture values risk-taking—defined as sharing new concepts and ideas—are five times more likely to excel at anticipating and responding to change effectively, and seven times more likely to innovate well than companies that are intolerant of risk-taking. In today's fast-changing markets, adapting quickly is essential to staying competitive, and many of the best-led companies intentionally nurture ecosystems that encourage their talent to challenge norms.[22]
- **Giving them a taste of good old management.** You can provide a lot of insight by letting your employees sample management. What might this involve? Well, you could take

---

[22]'Better pond, bigger fish', Deloitte., 2017, https://www2.deloitte.com/eg/en/pages/about-deloitte/articles/The-only-certainty-is-better-pond-bigger-fish.html, Accessed on 24 March 2022.

a day off and put someone in charge of the company while you're away (with certain limitations). You could introduce them to the systems you use to keep everything in line. You could pass them interesting hypotheticals about what they'd do in particular situations. The more they know about what it's like to work in management, the better at those tasks they'll become.

- **Providing them with training.** In their current role, it might not be possible for your future leaders to be exposed to areas that they need to develop. One example that comes to mind is commercial knowledge. Offering training that fills these knowledge gaps is a good way to help your staff develop. This could be done formally through an external training provider or informally through work-shadowing or internal coaching on specific skills and leadership competencies.

Takeaways

- Good leaders only focus on creating followers; exceptional leaders create new leaders.
- Budding leaders help you delegate tasks; they enable problem-solving, conflict resolution and reduce your stress.
- Budding leaders need you to tap their potential. Encourage their skills and leadership through coaching, mentoring and engaging with them emotionally.
- You can put your rising stars in situations where they have to multi-task or manage a team such that they can get a taste of what leadership really is. After all, practise makes perfect.
- Recognize their leadership potential and reward it so that you do not lose these star-performers.

12

CREATE A CULTURE THEY FALL IN LOVE WITH

If Aristotle were around in today's world and was asked to define organizational culture, he'd add two words to his famous quote: 'We are what we repeatedly do *at work*.'

'Culture eats strategy for breakfast,' is another famous quotation attributed to the late business management guru Peter Drucker. So, why exactly did Drucker make this statement? Because workplace culture is the practicing of an organization's values.

Some may believe that culture cannot be 'engineered', and that it just happens. It is true that culture happens whether you want it to or not. It is the company's DNA, and it is largely generated by the founders—not so much via their words as by their actions. So, by refusing to try to build a corporate culture, or even worse, by refusing to have company values, you are essentially choosing which culture will prevail—and this is often not for the better.

When it comes to attracting people and exceeding the competition, culture is a significant advantage. Almost half of employees would quit their current job for a lower-paying opportunity at a company with a superior culture, according to 77 per cent of workers who examine a company's culture before applying. The culture of an organization is also one of the top indicators of employee satisfaction and one of the main reasons that almost two-thirds of employees stay in their job.

Take, for example, Microsoft and Salesforce. Both technology-based organizations are world-class performers and well-known brands, thanks in part to their emphasis on culture. Satya Nadella, who took over as CEO of Microsoft in 2014, has successfully reformed Microsoft, which was once notorious for its ruthless competitiveness under Steve Balmer. He began a program to improve the company's culture, a process that shifted the emphasis away from competition and toward continual learning. Employees were urged to develop themselves rather than prove themselves. Microsoft's market capitalization is flirting with $1 trillion today, and it is once again contending with Apple and Amazon as one of the world's most valuable firms. Observe the power of a single leader and how they influenced the culture of a complete organization?

Yes, your company's culture affects nearly every area of your business, and you, as a leader, are the one in control of creating and maintaining it (with great power, comes great responsibility, remember?) A strong company culture can improve everything—from employee retention to the amount of revenue your organization generates. It's far more than just something your organization should have. It's critical to your organization's stability, longevity and perception.

You may ask, what exactly is this workplace culture? Workplace culture includes the qualities that make up a business and dictate how people within it should think, act and work together—as well as the physical working space of a firm.

Culture is the environment that surrounds us all the time. The shared values, belief systems, attitudes and set of assumptions that employees in a workplace share become a workplace culture. Individual upbringing, social and cultural context all influence this. However, in the workplace, leadership and strategic organizational directions and management have a significant impact on workplace culture. When a company's workplace culture is purposefully defined and actively worked on, the business thrives. Discord can occur when culture is left to its own devices.

A positive workplace culture fosters collaboration, boosts morale, boosts productivity and efficiency, and encourages employee retention. Workplace satisfaction, teamwork and productivity are all improved. Most essential, a nice work environment helps people to feel less stressed.

Here are some common myths about work culture you might want to dump in the trash can right away:

- A company's culture develops on its own and cannot be controlled.
- A company's culture is basically how employees talk to each other.
- Leaders cannot recreate a company's culture.
- A company's culture doesn't really affect workers' performance.
- Creating a strong work culture is too much of hassle, i.e., too much of spent money and time.
- Raising pays is good enough to keep workers happy.
- Setting a company's culture isn't a leader's responsibility.
- Company culture only includes fun activities and bonding between workers.

Now that you know workplace culture can be regulated and re-formed, go through the following factors that influence workplace culture:

- **Nature of the firm.** The purpose, market and operations of an organization have an impact on employees' behaviour. Does your organization make a meaningful difference through your products and services in the lives of your clients and customers? That has a direct impact on your organizational culture and how your employees feel about working for you.
- **Its people.** The people you hire—their personalities, beliefs, values, diverse skills and experiences, and everyday behaviours. The types of interactions that occur between employees (collaborative versus confrontational, supportive versus non-supportive, social versus task-oriented, etc.).
- **Its policies.** As far as leaders and employees embrace and abide by the organization's vision and mission statements, as well as the policies that support them, they can influence culture. An organization that wants to be more diverse and inclusive, for example, can pursue tactics to attract and retain more diverse employees. These ideals and rules would have a favourable impact on hiring practises and, as a result, workplace culture.
- **Its physical work environment.** Objects, artefacts and other physical signs at work. What workers put on their desks, what the organization hangs on its walls, how it allocates space and offices, how those offices appear (colour, furniture, etc.), and how common areas are used are all examples.
- **The external parties, including clients.** Why are clients a part of the culture? Because these are the people that directly affect the employee's well-being. If a customer is upset and takes it out on an employee, that employee's behaviour directly impacts those around them. If a client has a big success and thanks the employee for a job well done, that employee can uplift their whole team.
- **Workplace activities.** Practises related to recruiting,

selection, onboarding, compensation and benefits, rewards and recognition, training and development, advancement/promotion, performance management, wellness and work-life balance (paid time off, leave, etc.), as well as workplace traditions.

- **Lastly, and most importantly, *leadership*.** Even without realizing it, business leaders play a major part in influencing workplace culture. Employees in a company look up to its leaders and consider their actions as a model for how they should act. For example, if an organization declares that formal business attire is vital, but the leaders seldom dress formally, it will eventually be seen 'culturally acceptable' to dress more casually.

A positive business culture provides more than just a pleasant working environment. The success of an organization is determined by its culture. It may appear to be a no-brainer, but creating a vibrant workplace environment is more difficult than you might imagine. Policies, practises and people all play a role in creating the perfect workplace. When the infrastructure is in place, the advantages include higher productivity, increased revenue and a healthier workforce that is committed to organizational success.

A lot of research has shown that working in a positive environment has numerous benefits for individual employees and the business as a whole. Positive workplace culture is an uplifting atmosphere influenced by the values, beliefs, underlying assumptions, attitudes and behaviours shared by a group of people.

It's impossible to ensure that every employee is stress-free each day, but a positive work environment is one of the characteristics of organizational culture that thrives. A 2015 study published by *Behavioral Science & Policy* showed that employees were 50 per cent more likely to experience health problems in an uneasy or stressful work environment.[23] A healthy workplace culture translates to a healthier workforce. Organizations that care about their employees' personal and professional lives emphasize a zero-tolerance policy for bullying, a focus on work-life balance, and policies and procedures that promote a stress-free work environment. How does a positive workplace boost your employees' productivity?

- **Customer contentment.** A company with satisfied customers is a profitable company. You may wonder how internal culture could please customers. When your team is strong as a unit, it is better equipped to put forth exceptional work, create exceptional products and deliver exceptional service. The result: happy customers that stick around, keep buying, refer others and buy more per purchase.
- **Employee contentment.** 54 per cent of professionals base their career choices on finding a healthy work-life balance. The work-related stress epidemic is real and so is the desire to escape it. Employees, especially those with families, resent the idea of bringing work home with them. They do not want anything to intrude on their personal time with their loved ones. A corporate culture that embraces a healthy work-life balance through benefits—such as working remotely sometimes or giving employees the option to leave early in the summer on Fridays—will produce employees that come to work feeling refreshed and ready to take on the day.

---

[23]Joel Goh, Jeffrey Pfeffer and Stefanos A. Zenios, 'Workplace stressors & health outcomes: Health policy for the workplace', *Behavioral Science & Policy*, Vol. 1/1, Pp. 43–52, doi:10.1353/bsp.2015.0001.

- **And *your* contentment as a leader.** Most employees spend more time at work than they do with their families. Working in a stimulating, family-oriented environment is a pleasure rather than a chore. Employees are more productive when they are happy and feel important. Employees are enriched and encouraged to stay engaged by training, regular feedback, and rewards. Employees that feel valued provide tenfold to the organization, according to a healthy organizational culture. If this doesn't make a leader happy, what really does?
- **Attracting the cream of the cream like a magnet.** First impressions are everything when it comes to attracting and landing the best job applicants. 78 per cent of candidates say the hiring experience indicates how a company values its people. They are also drawn to working environments that incorporate clearly-defined values and a firm sense of purpose. These days, candidates have several ways to figure out if potential employers offer this type of environment—including employee reviews on websites such as Glassdoor. If your company culture is not conducive to showing employees they are valued, candidates will find this out and vice versa.
- **Retaining and motivating star players.** Do your employees wake up every day and look forward to a day of work or do they drag themselves to the workplace counting days to the weekend? Do they share your sense of ownership and commitment to the organization? The former can only be achieved in an environment that values human resources, treats people with trust and instils a sense of confidence and togetherness among employees. An organization that lacks a strong sense of loyalty and ownership among its personnel has a long way to go. An employee who genuinely cares about his or her company will spread the word and play a key role in attracting top talent to the company.

- **A great company image.** Word-of-mouth should never be underestimated—especially in the digital age. Your employees' social circles have expanded beyond their physical communities to include their online communities. As previously stated, Glassdoor allows anyone interested in working for your company to browse evaluations from current and former employees. The impact of a company's image isn't limited to that. Stakeholders and customers also use online review sites such as LinkedIn, Facebook, Google, Yelp and others to gauge their interest in doing business with organizations. The stronger your corporate culture is, the more likely employees are to speak positively about your company.

Redesign Your Office Space

Work productivity is linked to characteristics of the physical environment/culture of the workplace, such as ergonomic furniture, indoor air quality and lighting, in case you didn't know. Aside from the potential reduction in sick leave, enhancements to the physical environment can boost employee satisfaction and increase productivity.

The physical conditions you work under will play a crucial role in enabling you to reach your full potential. Ask yourself these questions and decide whether it's time to get a little creative with your workplace and redo it:

- How is the space allocated?
- Where are the offices located?
- How much space is given to whom?
- Are the light and temperature conducive?
- Is my office a little too bleak?

- What is posted on bulletin boards or displayed on walls?
- What is displayed on desks or in other areas of the building? In the work groups? On lockers or closets?
- How are common areas utilized?
- Is the furniture comfortable to use?
- Do your employees have access to refreshments and to each other?

1) **You might want to change your layout.** Some indoor workplaces have an open floor plan, while others use cubicles or other dividers to separate spaces. The nature of work determines how a workplace is designed. For example, an open layout may benefit a more collaborative setting, whereas a profession that requires discretion may benefit from separate offices or cubicles to maintain privacy.
2) **Let there be light.** Allow as much natural light as possible to enter. Sunlight has been shown to boost productivity, improve sleep quality and boost happiness. If you require window treatments, look into the finest options for letting light in while reducing glare on computer screens. Look outside to see if any trees need to be trimmed since they are blocking sunlight from the windows. Implement an open plan office to ensure that the largest amount of employees benefit from the natural light.
3) **A little green can never harm.** Sometimes less is less. There was a time when offices were expected to be as simple as possible. People are happier and more productive when they have house plants within sight of their workstation, according to research. 'If you are working in an environment where there's something to get you psychologically engaged you are happier and you work better', according to Dr Chris

Knight, who has been studying the subject for 10 years. He adds that other things could have the same effect as plants, like photographs or art.[24]

4) **Make it neat and tidy.** For some people, the office's cleanliness is a constant source of irritation. Germs spread rapidly in work spaces; thus, employees expect it to be thoroughly cleaned. Employers can help by offering keyboard wipes and desk cloths for employees who wish to keep their workspace clean. Make sure to address any trip hazards as soon as possible. Deliveries and boxes should be relocated to a storage place rather than being left behind the front desk or in the hallways. Spills should be cleaned as quickly as possible, and damaged floor coverings should be repaired or replaced.

There's nothing wrong with a little clutter, after all. It might even inspire you to be more creative. That does not, however, imply that you should work in a pigpen. Maintain a tidy and well-organized workspace. Not only will this save you time since you aren't searching for misplaced items, but it will also prevent your mind from zoning in on that mess.

5) **The right furniture.** Desks, chairs, conference tables and other workplace furniture can also impact employees on the job. Access to comfortable and adequate seating and functional desks can ensure indoor workplaces remain efficient. Outdoor workplaces may include comfortable furniture for break times. Human-centred workstations will keep employees healthier, happier and more productive.

---

[24]Shiv Malik, 'Plants in offices increase happiness and productivity', *The Guardian*, 1 September 2014, https://www.theguardian.com/money/2014/aug/31/plants-offices-workers-productive-minimalist-employees, Accessed on 24 March 2022.

Except for increasing the risk of premature death, bad sitting also causes musculoskeletal disorders, leading to less productivity and more sick leaves. You already know the effects of wrong posture on your poor back and neck all too well.

6) **The right facilities.** Office facilities can influence how you feel physically and mentally during your working life. Because being able to take a break or use the restroom is an important component of any productive daily routine—the location of these facilities can have an impact on the workplace. Additional amenities, such as relaxation rooms and on-site gyms, can have a good impact on your employees' energy levels.

7) **And don't forget the right tools.** It's almost impossible to get things done when you're not armed with the right tools, equipment and resources. Both you and your employees should have the right technology and tools needed to perform their duties. Furthermore, your team should be able to respond to any questions or complaints without having to jump through hoops. There should be cloud-based documents that address troubleshooting concerns, for example.

8) **Access to refreshments.** Hard time focusing? Struggling against sleep in front of the laptop? Everyone has been there. Workers' energy levels often drop at some points during the day. Refilling your coffee cup or attempting to boost oneself with something sugary is by far the most effective method. Regrettably, this does not improve your health at the same time. The most common cause of fatigue is a lack of water, therefore it's critical to provide employees with easy access to high-quality filtered water. To give your colleagues a greater opportunity of raising their energy levels

in a healthy and more effective method, replace harmful snacks in vending machines or cafes with nutritious snacks and supply baskets of fruits and vegetables.

9) **Hot 'n' Cold.** Some people are more sensitive to temperature than others. Workers have more control over their work environment when they use a local air conditioning system rather than a central system. Allow people to use small heaters or fans at their desks if they can't control the temperature.

10) **Check the acoustics.** The acoustics in a workplace plays a critical role in productivity and comfort. Researchers Robert Karasek and Lowel Tores Theorell have discovered that constant background noise disrupts learning, leads to fatigue and also increases stress hormones—therefore, quite bad for workers health.[25] Not only is too much noise dangerous, but too little noise can also be damaging. When you labour in complete silence, even the tiniest noises become distracting. A loud and chaotic setting, on the other hand, might feel overwhelming. Background noise similar to that found in cafés is widely believed to be ideal for a productive workplace. In open office landscapes, try to employ sound-absorbing surfaces, install separation walls, and provide areas where workers may communicate with each other or take phone calls without bothering others.

11) **Give employees *their* space, literally!** Allowing your employees to decorate their desks or cubicles with a photo or a child's drawing can make the difference between a sterile and a pleasant environment. Some employees will be delighted and calm if their workspace is personalized, while others may be unaffected.

---

[25] Robert Karasek and Lowel Tores Theorell, *Healthy Work: Stress, Productivity, and the Reconstruction Of Working Life,* Basic Books, 1992.

Make Your Work Culture Work (for Maximum Efficiency)

Leaders must understand their role in shaping an organization's culture, and organizations must make intentional efforts to help develop their leaders. Effective leadership development goes beyond training sessions to include things like adding to your organization's structure and establishing the correct cultural fit for new hires. Creating modern leaders is the best method to ensure that your leadership culture is positively contributing to your organizational culture.

The importance of leadership culture in the development of corporate culture cannot be overstated. The way leaders engage with one another and their team members is referred to as leadership culture. It's how leaders communicate, operate and make decisions. It's also about their daily work environment—including their behaviours, interactions, attitudes and values. Are the methods in which leadership shapes culture contributing to the culture you want to create? Is it helping you construct a strong corporate culture through the way they hire people, form high-performance teams, execute company strategy and engage their employees for the long haul?

1) **Ditch tradition, embrace modernity.** Instead of micromanaging and gatekeeping, modern leaders mentor and coach. Rather than trying to do everything themselves, they advocate for their employees and accomplish excellent work. Employees are valued, opportunities are provided and success is shared. Modern leaders are inherently inclusive and encourage their people to form bonds. Through frequent one-on-one conversations, leaders may make their people feel more connected. Leaders can use one-on-ones to check in with employees on a regular basis, give mentorship and

coaching, demonstrate appreciation and reinforce culture. Basically, you set an example for the entire team and organization to follow; you make or break it.
2) **Adopt team culture.** You already know that in today's competitive world, you need to assemble a strong team. When you put a group of high-performing employees together to establish a team where their skills can be combined, magic happens. Not only will they have a lot of positive energy, but their performance, loyalty and engagement will improve significantly. So, once you've found the best employees for your team and aligned them with their purpose, you'll have a high-performing group focused on something bigger than themselves. Ensure that you:

- Make teamwork your company's core value.
- Meet regularly with your staff as this can make a big difference in great team culture.
- Communicate clearly with team members, so everyone is on the same page.
- Provide constructive feedback to help your team improve.
- Celebrate birthdays, promotions and holidays with your team.
- Promote a culture of learning where every employee is encouraged to continue expanding their skill sets.

3) **Balance it out.** When possible, give top staff members the option to follow a flexible schedule or telecommute one day a week. It doesn't cost anything to implement these changes, and employees will appreciate the leeway as well as the opportunity to achieve better balance.
4) **Respect diversity.** Creating a working environment where each employee's individuality and uniqueness can play a

role comes with a number of benefits. You'll promote a working environment in which all employees can display their maximum potential and unleash their creativity.

5) **Check up on your staff.** Contrary to popular belief, creating a positive work environment for your team doesn't have to be complicated. In fact, 39 per cent of American workers say regular check-ins are the number-one thing that makes them feel happy at the office, according to a recent EY survey.[26] Pay a visit to your colleagues' desks and solicit their opinions. Alternatively, if you have a remote workforce, send an informal message to them. Then, by following up, you may demonstrate that you care. You'll be astonished at how much these modest activities may increase productivity across an organization—regardless of where an individual works.

6) **Acknowledge and reward good work.** Workplace culture is not just about changing the behaviour of your workforce—it is about how you act at your workplace. Appreciate and reward excellent performance. Employees have tight timetables and a long list of jobs to do before deadlines. As a result, when employees go above and beyond, as a leader, you should acknowledge and praise them. This is the first step toward creating a positive workplace culture that values hard work. Employees are boosted by this behaviour, which drives them to do better in the future.

7) **Give feedback.** Your leadership development program may collapse before it has a chance to thrive if you don't provide regular constructive feedback. Tell your future leaders how

---

[26]Karyn Twaronite, 'Five findings on the importance of belonging', EY, 11 May 2019, https://www.ey.com/en_us/diversity-inclusiveness/ey-belonging-barometer-workplace-study, Accessed on 24 March 2022.

they're doing, and provide them praise and guidance to help them along the way. They'll be eager to learn if they're doing a good job, and if there are any areas where they can improve or grow. Feedback can help you figure out if there are any problems or if you need to adjust the pace or structure of their development early on.

8) *And* **take it too.** First, you need to collect feedback using the right listening tools that make it easy for employees to express what they're feeling in the moment—like pulse surveys and workplace chatbots. Then analyse the results to see what's working and what isn't in your organization; and act on those findings while they're still relevant. This not only strengthens your culture, but it also has other benefits, such as increased employee satisfaction and profitability. According to a survey, 68 per cent of employees who receive regular feedback are satisfied with their positions, while another study discovered that companies with managers who receive feedback on their strengths are 8.9 per cent more profitable. In addition to gathering feedback using the methods described above, make sure you're paying attention to more subtle expressions of feedback that can reveal cultural deficiencies. For example, pay attention to body language, as it can tell you a lot—even when employees aren't willing to share. If you're working with a remote team, video conferences can help keep this nonverbal channel of communication open. Managers should treat all their sessions with employees as opportunities to gather and respond to feedback and act as a trusted coach.

9) **Be a techy.** Today, access to digital tools can make a massive difference in how we work. Employees will feel that their time is being wasted in organizations that continue to use outdated, manual methods of working. Digital

transformation might make or break your workplace culture as Gen Z (the first completely digitally native generation) enters the workforce. Companies can use workflow automation to relieve employee stress, allowing them to innovate, learn new skills, take time off, start a side hustle, or engage in other more meaningful activities. I'll tell you more on this in the next chapter; don't take a reading break yet!

10) **Your budding leaders have to set the culture too.** The future success of your firm—in terms of building a meaningful workplace culture—is in the hands of your budding team leaders and managers. If your workplace culture stresses certain values, but your leadership team does not represent them—or even displays behaviours that contradict them, the effort is undermined. The dissonance between proclaimed values and lived behaviours will be recognized by team members. They may even begin to imitate negative actions, because they believe management has rewarded them for them. Employees, on the other hand, would automatically follow suit for more recognition if they see rising stars and budding leaders embodying your culture (and even being rewarded for it).

Takeaways

- As a leader, you're responsible for setting the entire company's culture.
- A firm's culture not only includes values, ethics and working patterns but is also reflected in the way its physical workspace functions.
- Redo your office to optimize your staff's convenience, comfort and productivity.

- Create a culture that prioritizes teamwork, collaboration and communication. Lone wolves cannot create empires.
- In this culture, make sure you appreciate hard work, guide employees if they mess up and provide other material benefits too.
- Lastly, as a leader, you have to *live* your company's culture.

13

THE POST-PANDEMIC LEADER: YOUR BRAND-NEW LEADERSHIP STYLE

> *The thing that's been positively surprising to people is that people are more productive working at home than people would have expected. Some people thought that everything was just going to fall apart, and it hasn't. And a lot of people are actually saying that they're more productive now.*[27]
>
> —Mark Zuckerberg, CEO of Facebook

No one could have predicted the drastic shift Covid-19 would bring to the American workforce. Every employee who was able to make the shift to remote work did so almost immediately, and for many of us, it has become a permanent arrangement. The coronavirus outbreak was dubbed 'The world's largest work-from-home experiment' by Time magazine. This appears to be a long-term experiment based on the numbers. The

---

[27] Casey Newton, 'Mark Zuckerberg on Taking His Massive Workforce Remote', *The Verge*, 21 May 2020, https://www.theverge.com/2020/5/21/21265780/facebook-remote-work-mark-zuckerberg-interview-wfh, Accessed on 25 March 2022.

demand for excellent virtual leadership abilities has never been greater, with so many people continuing to work from home.

Whether you're a new manager or a seasoned CEO, you'll need to make several adjustments and alterations to your leadership techniques as you move from in-person to virtual leadership. You already know the global, transformational and modern leading is adaptive and situational: our situation today demands you to adapt to new forms of technology and becoming a virtual leader. Guess what? The time to change is *now*.

Research shows that moving to a virtualized world puts leadership skills to the test. Evidence reveals that leaders must be on their A-game all of the time if they want their teams and communities to perform well when working independently.

This is the new normal, regardless of how well prepared you were to work from home for over a year. Leading remote teams and being a part of a completely remote team can produce significant signs of overwhelm, stress and burnout if not handled effectively. There are, fortunately, ways to avoid this.

Virtual leadership is a type of management that takes place in a remote working environment. Virtual leaders, like traditional leaders, focus on motivating employees and assisting teams in achieving their objectives. Virtual leaders must take a different management approach compared to leading in an office—as team communication isn't done in person but rather through online and virtual mediums. As such, virtual leaders need a different skill set to leaders in an office setting. The pandemic has forced much of the workforce into remote working, and for many employees, this is the first time they have tried working from home.

In addition, the way leaders now interact with employees has changed. Virtual leaders can't check in with workers the same way in-office managers do, so they have to put their trust in their workers' capabilities.

- Your employees save time and energy on their daily commute.
- They avoid the distractions and pressures of a traditional office environment.
- Work during non-traditional hours when they feel most productive. (for the night-owls out there)
- You can hire new talent from anywhere and everywhere.
- Say hello to global customers and clients.
- Think about this logically: you save a massive amount of expenditure on office infrastructure and equipment.

Although remote functioning of teams probably gives you the jitters, you may want to know how remote working teams can be more successful:

How then, do you become the perfect virtual leader loved by all even amidst chaos and crisis?

- **Stay connected.** Remote work is often associated with social isolation. People feel they are no longer a part of the team, they miss communicating with co-workers, and a strong sense of loneliness develops with time. To avoid falling into this trap, organize group chats or a combined lunch session with some of your co-workers with your cameras turned on. It's critical for remote leaders to check in with each of their direct reports at least once a week to preserve a sense of belonging and to maintain (or improve) trust levels with their team members. In David Rabin's words, 'There is nothing more important in a group remote project than casual communication. Not just official emails and work updates, but the ability to sit back and chat.'
- ***But*** **also let go a little.** As a leader, you have to trust your employees, irrespective of if you're in-person with them or

remote. But as a remote leader, that trust becomes even more paramount. 'Building trust and rapport across the team,' according to remote managers, is the most important thing for new managers to focus on (33 percent of remote managers indicated this) and what new managers most frequently overlook (25 percent of remote managers said this).

So what if someone walks out and runs to the store in the middle of the day? If someone takes the afternoon off to go watch their kid's school play, what then? In fact, it's great that they get to do those things, live their life and get work done too. It doesn't matter how many hours are being put into the work or when the work is being done. All that matters are the results—and I trust our employees to find a way to make the results happen.

- **Try meeting your team 'face-to-face'.** Consistent, open communication is a common difficulty with remote teams, so you must put in a little extra work to make that happen while your team is temporarily remote. Put at least one weekly video conferencing meeting on the calendar—you can call it a check-in, an update or a status meeting—and devote that time to project management, providing your team with any pertinent updates, seeing how they are doing with their work—as well as personally—and taking questions.
- **Don't leave anyone out.** If you manage a large team or are responsible for your entire organization, make sure that you are checking in with *everyone*—not just the people you interact with on a daily basis. This may include administrators, IT personnel, support staff or janitorial workers. This will go a long way in boosting morale and giving you insight from all levels of the company.

- **Set clear but achievable goals and expectations.** Working remotely offers employees greater flexibility—not only on where they live but also on the exact hours they work. For example, some employees may prefer to work later in the day and take a longer lunch, so that they can work out or take their dog for a walk.

  Virtual leaders should be aware of this and not set unrealistic expectations. When teams are not physically in the same location, often the best way to measure an employee's performance is through outcomes and goal completion. Specifically, measurable goals are crucial, and tracking them frequently can help to ensure team members stay on track and that the team leader is able to identify problems before they become catastrophic.
- **Use appropriate channels to communicate.** Discuss when it's appropriate to use instant message, email and webcam meetings. Understand when a meeting is necessary versus a quick announcement. No one likes attending hour-long meetings when the question could be addressed more efficiently in an email. At the same time, no one likes discussing important and urgent issues through dry emails. That's when you instead use instant messaging and video conferencing tools such as Zoom, Microsoft Teams, Google Meet, Skype or Facetime. God bless technology, right?
- **Lead with compassion.** To be an excellent virtual leader, you need to get in touch with your team members at an emotional level, and be completely honest and transparent when sharing data and status updates (even unfavourable information) in order to maintain trust. Check in with your team individually to see how they're doing—particularly as some may find adjusting to remote work difficult. Ask about their families, their hobbies or something interesting

they saw on social media. Empathize with them to show a shared understanding—letting them know that you see them as a *person*, not just an employee. The post-pandemic leader understands how the pandemic has caused an emotional, mental and physical burnout for most of their employees; the post-pandemic leader treats his team like human beings first and workers next.
- **Encourage socialization between teammates.** For remote workers, isolation can have a huge impact on productivity and motivation. Taking a few minutes before team meetings for casual talk might be a simple way to encourage social engagement. Catch up with everyone, talk about Netflix shows and look into common interests. You may even arrange virtual parties by having food brought to each remote team member during a video conversation for special occasions. Create a watercooler channel or chatroom on your favourite messaging app for a 24/7 outlet. Such exchanges, which range from arguing sports to sharing the latest memes, help to improve team relationships and lift morale. After all, you've got to work with what you've got, right?
- **Use various online tools to the max.** Making appropriate use of collaborative software is one of the main principles of effective leadership in virtual teams. Choosing a project management tool that is right for your company, getting everyone on board, and using it to properly distribute tasks and measure progress is a wonderful way to stay organized as a virtual team. You can use Trello, Asana, Monday or a time-tracking software like Time Doctor to ace meeting those dreadful deadlines.

Know your technology and don't rely on just one to interact with team members. For example, email is frequently regarded as the least interesting method of forming teams.

The best method is to use virtual conferencing, but consider meeting in small groups. Large virtual meetings can easily become disorganized and unproductive. Audio conferencing calls are good for quick meetings, but if sensitive information needs to be discussed, video conferences are the way to go. Live chat apps should be used for time-sensitive communications.

Takeaways

- The meaning of leadership has changed radically after the Covid-19 Pandemic. The adaptable leader is naturally the virtual leader.
- Virtual leading isn't as hard or tedious as it may seem: it saves costs and can lead to boosted employee productivity, if done right.
- A virtual leader is well-versed with technology, empathetic and engaged with his/her team.
- A virtual leader enables socialization between team-members through informal meetings and online celebrations.
- Virtual leadership understands the various aspects of technology; different tools and different modes of communication are to be used for varying purposes—depending upon the time, situation, employees and the type of project.